Polina Bardaeva

Bank Asset Liability Management Best Practice

The Moorad Choudhry Global Banking Series

Series Editor
Professor Moorad Choudhry

Polina Bardaeva

Bank Asset Liability Management Best Practice

Yesterday, Today and Tomorrow

DE GRUYTER

The views, thoughts and opinions expressed in this book represent those of the author in her individual private capacity, and should not in any way be attributed to any employing institution, or to the author as a director, representative, officer, or employee of any affiliated institution. While every attempt is made to ensure accuracy, the author or the publisher will not accept any liability for any errors or omissions herein. This book does not constitute investment advice and its contents should not be construed as such. Any opinion expressed does not constitute a recommendation for action to any reader. The contents should not be considered as a recommendation to deal in any financial market or instrument and the authors, the publisher, the editor, any named entity, affiliated body or academic institution will not accept liability for the impact of any actions arising from a reading of any material in this book.

ISBN 978-3-11-066654-0
e-ISBN (PDF) 978-3-11-066976-3
e-ISBN (EPUB) 978-3-11-066660-1
ISSN 2627-8847

Library of Congress Control Number: 2021930876

Bibliographic information published by the Deutsche Nationalbibliothek
The Deutsche Nationalbibliothek lists this publication in the Deutsche Nationalbibliografie; detailed bibliographic data are available on the internet at http://dnb.dnb.de.

Cover image: Nikada/E+/Getty Images
Typesetting: Integra Software Services Pvt. Ltd.
Printing and binding: CPI books GmbH, Leck

www.degruyter.com

To my parents

Acknowledgments

First of all, I want to thank my parents, Elena and Sergey; they defined who I am, my principles, understanding of right and wrong, how to set aims and how to achieve them. You have always believed that I can exceed my goals and that inspires me to new achievements. All my success I owe to you! Thank you for your love and devotion.

I was very lucky to have Oxana Baydina as my university supervisor. Thank you a lot – for taking me on this journey called academic work, educating me on how to structure thoughts, stimulating my own research, helping me with always relevant advice and supporting me in times when I got stuck and didn't know how to continue. I want to thank also my alma mater Moscow State University for opening the doors to my professional life.

I would like to thank those who actually brought me into the ALM management profession – Timofey Kovalkov and Mikhail Toporov. Thank you for your enthusiasm and full involvement in this topic, and for showing me this area of banking, with which I fell in love at first sight.

And if there is a person, about whom I can say that without him this book would never be a reality, that is Moorad Choudhry. I can describe this only as a miracle, that I was able to actually meet the person whom I admired while writing my PhD thesis, but also that he gave me the chance to cooperate with him in his projects! A big thank you for this opportunity, as well as for your motivating support, and for setting really high quality targets and leading by example in meeting them.

I also extend my thanks to all my colleagues from Sberbank Europe AG (especially to Kornel Halmos, Ivan Mirgorodskiy, Leonhard Riebl, Aleksandr Mikayelyan and Peter Niemiec for the constantly appearing ALM challenges which we discuss and solve together) and also to my ex-colleagues and friends, including Yulia Zaytseva, Massimo Pedroni, the BTRM team (Edward Bace, Chris Wescott, Chris Uduezue, Werner Coetzee), and Sberbank of Russia Treasury (in particular Alexey Lyakin, Iya Malakhova, Maria Volozhinskaya, Anton Sorokin, Elena Chistyakova, Alexandr Letunov).

Thank you to Anuk Teasdale for undertaking the first and the most hard proof read and to the De Gruyter editorial team, and especially to Jaya Dalal, for always having an optimal solution with regards to the book. I'm also thankful to Mervin Ebenezer and Integra Software Services for handling the production of the book.

Finally, I'm very happy to have Andrey Kurdyumov in my life, to whom I say thank you for being here, and for making me confident in what I'm doing and in the "happily ever after."

https://doi.org/10.1515/9783110669763-202

Foreword

This is a very timely, topical and comprehensive exposition of asset and liability management (ALM) for financial institutions by Dr. Bardaeva. It builds substantially upon prior works, including the 2007 volume by Professor Moorad Choudhry and her own 2011 text, but expands considerably upon the all-important function of ALM and the overriding imperative for it to be firmly established in financial institution processes and procedures. The author, currently heading Group Capital Management for Sberbank Europe AG, brings her decades of banking and ALM experience solidly to the fore in outlining current best practice and in looking forward to a sustainable future for the industry. She is prescient in her ability to identify and suggest benefits from new and emerging trends in innovative ALM practices.

As a faculty member colleague in the Bank Treasury Risk Management programme (BTRM), I have regularly observed and learned from her, as she most ably embeds and reinforces high standards of professional practice in ALM among numerous cohorts of bank practitioners at all levels. She very rightly focuses in this opus on key fundamentals such as the crucial significance of the balance sheet, the treasury operating model, the salient relationships that exist between it and the risk, market and finance functions, and she thoroughly covers the Supervisory Review and Evaluation Process gaining ever more attention among regulators. This discussion extends significantly and in a holistic manner to relevant considerations of governance, capital, liquidity and funding. The regulatory aspect is indeed amply explored, with very useful suggestions as to how to optimise this dynamic. Particularly compelling is the incisive discussion around the wider role that ALM plays in response to new challenges to the industry, as well as conflicts of interest to be avoided. In this accomplished and clearly written work Dr. Bardaeva further demonstrates her expertise in constructing the internal yield curve for an institution, which has critical implications for profitability.

This book is a highly noteworthy addition to the growing corpus of literature on best practice in the banking industry, and the too often overlooked area of ALM. It is to be warmly welcomed by both professional and academic practitioners in the field, as well as by those who are simply just setting forth on their ALM journey. I heartily recommend it.

Dr. Edward Bace
Middlesex University Business School
5 January 2021

https://doi.org/10.1515/9783110669763-203

Contents

Preface

When looking back at the history of banking, in almost every decade the banking business has faced dramatic changes. Bankers, who successfully survived one or more banking crises, start to think that they have learned the lessons from the past as they incorporated abounding and complicated mechanisms in their usual banking activities. But then one more crisis comes along and threatens the bank's sustainability again. Why are we still so exposed to negative external implications? And what can we do to protect ourselves and our banks from new shocks? And will we ever return to the 3-6-3 principle, when bankers left the office at 3 p.m. to play golf (see interpretation in Chapter 1)?

I believe that as long as a dominant approach across banking addresses problems separately, banks will be failing to confirm the viability of their business in the long run. The crucial point in banking is understanding the interconnections between its areas. Asset and liability management (ALM) stands exactly at the crossroads of almost all banking functions, and its impact should never be understated. Proper and timely ALM involvement in banks' processes significantly increases the efficiency of the entire bank. The ALM discipline embraces not only the setting of balance sheet targets, instruments, and methodologies to achieve the goals, but also a correct, holistic understanding of procedures that should be set up in a bank to prove the ongoing continuity of its operations and compliance with internal and external constraints. In this book my aim is to show that if undertaken correctly, ALM will almost rule the bank, enabling the bank to fulfill its mission, to be in line with regulatory requirements and to maintain long-term financial health.

After working for 15 years in ALM, mastering my skills in one or another ALM topic and sharing them with my students, I have concluded that ALM is not just a set of methods and instruments (although it is very important to know these). Its dedication goes much further. In contrast to many previously published books on bank ALM, this text provides the philosophy of ALM, describes how through time it has adapted to a changing environment and become more involved in steering the bank. This book raises the question of interrelation of processes inside the bank, suggesting that we manage the bank almost as a human organism, considering that a change in one item would also impact other areas. It also suggests that improving one banking function will positively influence the entire bank.

This book also presents one idea from the first page to the last, which is to underline the importance of the interconnection of all banking processes evolving around ALM. Although the book contains interpretations and descriptions of separate ALM phenomena and best practices related to them, its real objective is to show how the methodological base for each ALM topic contributes to the overall picture; something that ALM managers must keep in front of their eyes at all times to ensure a consistent steering of the bank.

https://doi.org/10.1515/9783110669763-205

This book will be of value to those who want to understand the basics of ALM, notwithstanding their level of expertise, as one should always refer to the history of the issue to understand the roots and the reasons for its successes and failures. I hope the picture of ALM practice presented in this book will inspire students and other banking specialists, as I was once inspired myself, to choose ALM or interconnected spheres for their career development. This book may also be worthy of the attention of senior management, to enable them to get a deeper understanding of possible conflicts of interest in banks, subsequent solutions, new challenges for different types of banks, and how ALM can be helpful in overcoming them.

All ideas and considerations described in this book are those of the author alone and do not reflect the views of the entities to which the author is or has been associated.

Polina Bardaeva
Vienna
10 October 2020

Part 1: Historical Asset and Liability Management Concepts

Various changes in financial markets adjust banking activities and impact the structure of the balance sheets. It all leads to modification of the tasks in asset and liability management (ALM). And logically, for solving different tasks at different times in the past various methods and ALM instruments were applied. As tasks, methods, and instruments constitute a concept, we can speak about changing ALM concepts over time. In what follows, is a description of retrospective ALM concepts and their development over time, together with a summary table showing the main characteristics of the concepts and the reason for the changes.

This part answers the following questions:
- How have the ALM tasks and aims developed over time?
- What has triggered every change of the ALM aim?
- When and why have well-known instruments, methods, and approaches appeared?
- What is the interconnection between the ALM concepts?

The definition of ALM, as ALM is considered now, will be offered first in the second part of the book. This is done intentionally, as not all the tasks that are now commonly assigned to the ALM appeared at once. As a response to the changing external conditions, banking activities and balance sheet items (as well as their proportion in the balance sheet) have been changing over time, setting new priorities and tasks for the ALM. The breadth of the new tasks increased as new methods and instruments and their combinations appeared. It also happened as a response to new challenges, regulatory updates, and research for mitigation measures after severe crises. In order to present the development of ALM in a more structural way, I suggest splitting ALM tasks in the following areas:[1]

1. Management of ALM risks
2. Setting targets for the balance sheet structure
3. Defining the price benchmarks
4. Allocation of financial resources between business lines

At the same time each ALM area could be split into a short-term part, aiming to solve tactical tasks, which are executed on an everyday basis, and a long-term one. The latter is represented by strategic tasks, long lasting projects, resulting in months' or even years' time. They can also be split into two parts as well: the "going concern" – when the bank continues to develop according to its strategy, and the "gone concern" – when a crisis comes and banks need to execute specific measures to recover from it.

1 This split is explicitly covered in Part 2 of the book, together with descriptions of each task and definition of ALM overall.

https://doi.org/10.1515/9783110669763-001

Chapter 1
Before the ALM Era

There's a well-known joke, that in the beginning of the second half of the XX century, banking business operated according to a "3-6-3 principle." Its main rules were "raise money at 3%, lend money at 6%, and after 3 p.m. bankers should go to play golf." No one ever thought about any risks (ALM risks), pricing was simple and required no benchmarking, resources were not that scarce to be cautiously allocated within business lines (the business lines, though, also hardly existed at that time), and requirements in the way we know them now were far from their emergence. The world was recovering from the war, production was developing, banks were actively lending to companies and individuals.

From the ALM point of view this period does not deserve much attention, as the ALM almost did not exist at that time. The aim of banks and those managers who were responsible for matching asset and liability sides of the balance sheet was *stable margin.*[2] It was achieved by means of thorough planning of loans and funding volumes in the long run, balancing mismatches by interbank borrowing and placements, cash, and equivalents management – as a part of operational activities.

Nevertheless, the volumes on the asset and liability sides were compared according to their contractual time to maturity – so one can already speak of preliminary liquidity management and *liquidity risk management*. Additional argument toward the fact that banks took tenors into account is already invented misbalance analysis methods for assets and liabilities; for example, duration analysis method was suggested by Macauley[3] in 1938 and was further enhanced by Redington[4] in 1952.

Allocation of interest margin between the lending and deposit raising divisions was made, according to a "single pool approach." Banks used a single internal rate (the ancestor of the current funds transfer pricing [FTP] rate and curve) and applied it to calculate the margins on assets and liabilities. The difference between asset rate offered to a customer and the single internal rate (multiplied by volume) represented the result of the lending division, the difference between the single internal rate and the liability rate offered to a customer (also multiplied by volume) represented the financial result of the fundraising division. It means that interest expense or interest

2 This conclusion is supported in many sources on banking that time, for example, John F. Marshall and Vipul K. Bansal, *Financial Engineering: A Complete Guide to Financial Innovation.* New York Institute of Finance, 1991.

3 F.R. Macauley, *Some Theoretical Problems Suggested by the Movements of Interest Yields, Bond Yields & Stock Prices in the United States Since 1856*, Reprint Edition. Ayer Co. Pub., 1981.

4 F.M. Redington, "Review of the Principles of Life Office Valuations," *Journal of the Institute of Actuaries* 78, 1952, 286–340.

https://doi.org/10.1515/9783110669763-002

income was allocated in a way as though assets and liabilities of businesses were equal, with the same maturities.[5]

Having no evidence of other, more sophisticated methods and instruments to be applied, ALM intervention in the banking activities was at its minimum level (that is why the concept can be called *minimum intervention*), the picture of the ALM tasks is represented in Table 1.1.

Table 1.1: Minimum intervention ALM concept (1950–1973).

1950–1973		ALM risk management	BS structure targeting	Price benchmarking	Resources allocation
Short-term/ tactical tasks		Operational liquidity management Cash and equivalents management Interbank placements Exchange operations			
Long-term/ strategic tasks	**Going concern**	Liquidity risk management	Volumes planning*		

*Today, volumes planning is not considered as an ALM task (it is fully in the area of responsibilities of business lines), but as ALM did not actually exist then – and executed a mixture of controlling and trading functions – it can be counted for the ALM task at that time.

5 A more detailed description can be found in the article by D.R. van Deventer, "Transfer Pricing Systems Design: Building Clarity in the Responsibility for and Measurement of Risk." https://www.kamakuraco.com/banking/ftp/

Chapter 2
Financial Turbulence

Change of ALM tasks and priorities happened in the first half of the 1970s, as a result of different worldwide events. U.S. President Richard Nixon trying to curb increasing inflation in the country undertook a series of economic measures. One of them was a breakage of the dollar's link to gold and turning the American dollar into a freely floating currency. By this measure the Bretton Woods system was eliminated, and starting from 1973 the current regime based on freely floating fiat currencies came in place. Although freeing of the dollar resulted in its further devaluation and higher inflation inside the country. Also, Western European countries that were still holding dollars in their state savings faced revaluation of budgets. In addition to the effects of the Bretton Woods' system crash and devaluation of the dollar the oil crisis in 1973 impacted Western European countries: as OPEC members proclaimed an oil embargo, prices of oil had risen tremendously, by nearly 400% within a year, according to the Office of the Historian of the U.S. Department of State.[1]

Higher inflation, due to these severe events, led to increase of interest rates, unexpected by market participants and never experienced before. The banks and savings associations (retail banks analogues) faced a problem of maturity mismatch between assets (mainly long-term mortgage loans disbursed at fixed rates) and liabilities (short-term retail deposits). Abrupt rising of interest rates at that time increased the funding costs (the short-term liabilities were renewed at higher rates), but at the same time the average long-term loan portfolio rates stayed at the previous level. Thus, the banks faced a significant drop of their profit as a result of interest rate risk (IRR) realization.

This caused the banks to reconsider the ALM aim, as the first priority a task to *close all the gaps* and to minimize financial risks was defined. Although there are many classifications of financial risks, in this chapter financial risks are comprised of mainly IRR and liquidity risk, but, as it is proven in theoretical studies and practical business cases, all the risks are interconnected and can be a cause of another risk type.

As a response to the external changes and necessity to return stability to banks and financial systems, ALM methods and instruments were enhanced by those methods and instruments, which we know are used to decrease or eliminate the risk.[2] The

1 Milestones in the History of U.S. Foreign Relations: OPEC Oil Embargo 1973–1974, Office of the Historian of the U.S. Department of State.

2 K. Mitchell, "Interest Rate Risk Management at Tenth Distinct Banks," *Economic Review*. The Federal Reserve Bank of Kansas City, May 1985.

https://doi.org/10.1515/9783110669763-003

following measures and instruments were introduced to eliminate the risk that interest spread would shorten:
- Decrease of planned/budgeted volumes of mortgage loans
- Rollover of old loans by substituting them with new ones at market rates
- Lending loans at floating interest rates
- Selling of mortgage loan portfolios at the secondary market (later for such aims securitization will be applied)
- Substitution of saving deposits and on demand accounts by more flexible deposits at floating rates
- Development and introduction of individual programs for deposit raising

As it can be seen from the list above, the ALM methods and instruments used for risk minimization in banks were impacting the balance sheet structure and banks' balance sheet parameters and characteristics. During this period, application of balance sheet methods and instruments for ALM was reflected in numerous articles that confirmed the actuality of such methods. For example, in working papers of Toshia Masuoka[3] it is emphasized that increased volatility of exchange rates after the transition to the floating exchange rates system in 1973 triggered the necessity to develop and apply the balance sheet methods and instruments for ALM. Masuoka defined the major ALM task at the end of the 1980s as a systematic control of price risk, which could lead to unexpected decreases of banks' net interest income as a result of interest rate changes, so balance sheet instruments could help to avoid or overcome this risk. Masuoka also mentioned other measures and presented them in the following classification: (a) instruments of self-insurance (balance sheet instruments); (b) instruments of third party insurance (e.g., derivatives); and (c) all other instruments (external instruments), but other authors at that time concluded that derivatives were not used overall everywhere, as for ALM tasks balance-sheet instruments were considered as sufficient.

The main balance sheet approaches could be observed in all areas of ALM. As it was outlined previously, *to manage ALM risks* an approach of maturity matching was applied. Not only was the liquidity gap analyzed and closed, but also the interest rate decomposition of asset and liability maturities was considered. The main difference between liquidity gap and interest rate gap analysis is that in liquidity gap cash flows are considered at the actual time, when the cash flow happens, whereas in the interest rate gap analysis the volumes are reflected at the earliest of either actual maturity date or the date of the floating interest rate repricing. The banks aimed to match the maturities in the long run in the interest rate gap analysis and in the short run via cash flows analysis.

3 T. Masuoka, "Asset and Liability Management in the Developing Countries: Modern Financial Techniques – A Primer," The World Bank Working Paper, No. 454, June 1990.

A short numerical example below aims to show the differences between two types of gaps.

Box 2.1. Difference Between Liquidity and Interest Rate Gaps

In general, liquidity and interest rate gaps serve different purposes. Whereas the liquidity gap is used for assessing physical liquidity needs, the interest rate gap indicates impact of interest rate repricing on the net interest margin of the bank.

Let's consider an example (Table 2.1), when a bank has only the following assets and liabilities:

Table 2.1: Simplified example of a bank's balance sheet.

	Amount	Tenor	Rate type
Asset 1	10	1M	fixed
Asset 2	25	6M	fixed
Asset 3	30	1Y	3M float
Asset 4	35	2Y	fixed
Liability 1	10	3M	fixed
Liability 2	30	1Y	fixed
Liability 3	60	2Y	6M float

In order to construct liquidity gap one should place assets as inflows and liabilities as outflows (volumes with a negative sign) at dates of their contractual (or anticipated) maturity (column "Tenor"). A simple gap at each time represents comparison of inflows and outflows, shows if there are enough inflows and stock to cover the outflows, and should be used for operational liquidity management. In order to assess the liquidity position on a longer time horizon, a measure of cumulative gap is applied. It shows whether at some future moment the cumulative amount of inflows may not be enough to cover the outflows. As it can be seen in Figure 2.1, constructed based on numbers of the example, liquidity for

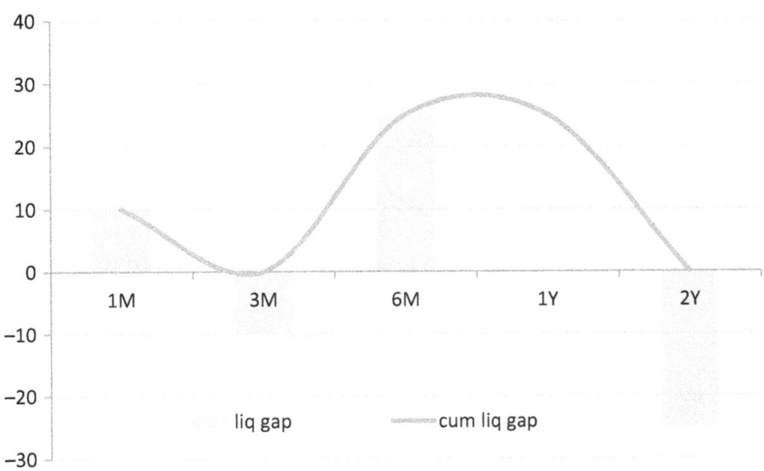

Figure 2.1: Liquidity gap.

this bank at all times is kept above the zero level, meaning, that no additional funds should be raised at any of the tenors to ensure execution of outflows (of course, unless the picture changes).

At the same time, the situation looks unsatisfactory while speaking about the interest rate gap. In order to construct an interest rate gap one should place assets as inflows and liabilities as outflows (volumes with a negative sign) at dates of their maturity (column "Tenor"), if their interest rate is fixed, and at dates of the interest rate repricing (column "Rate type"), if the interest rate is floating. The cumulative gap represents amounts at risk of repricing with negative implications for the bank.

Cumulative interest rate gap shows (Figure 2.2) that if rates go down in the next one to three months, then placement assets (which will mature at that time and will need to be placed again) will be made at lower rates than before. While liabilities are not yet repriced, it will negatively impact the interest rate margin. At the same time, the graph also shows, that if in six months to a year the rates go up, the bank's liabilities will reprice, again negatively impacting banks' profitability.

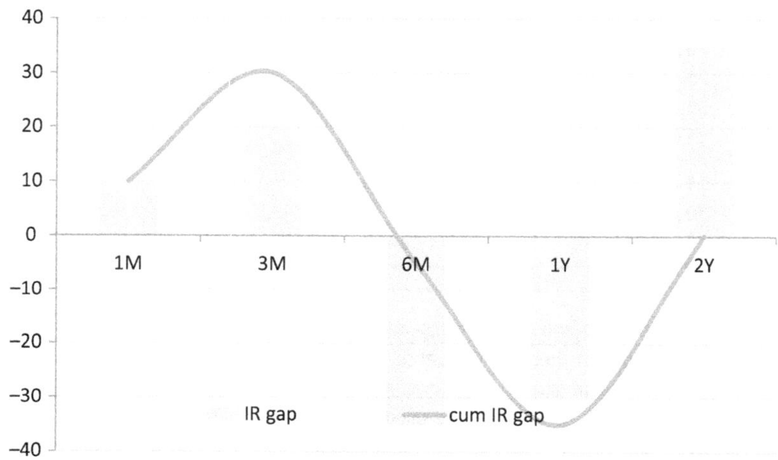

Figure 2.2: Interest rate gap.

Thus, whereas liquidity gap is preferably to be positive at all times, the interest rate gap ideally should be kept around a zero level, or at any times within the set on it in the risk appetite statement (RAS) (see Part 2) levels.

It was still within ALM to plan the volumes as an approach of *the balance sheet structure targeting*, but in comparison to the previous period not only in terms of increasing either volumes of assets, or volumes of liabilities, but also through active changing of the maturity of either of the balance sheet sides: through rollovers, prepayments, selling and buying of portfolios and single loans, granting individual conditions for faster and better raising of deposits. At that time better diversification of funding sources took place. Long-term debt issuances became more popular, including the ones at floating rates.

With the introduction of floating rates and new balance sheet measures (as repayment and portfolio selling) there was not enough done with regard to the *price benchmarking and the FTP*. The risk mitigation approach (when volumes of different portfolios on the asset and liability sides were balanced) again enabled only one internal rate for each portfolio for splitting the interest rate margin between different banking lines. These internal interest rates were used on a "non-prepayable" basis, assuming that the prepayment (before maturity) does not impact the result of the deal. Of course, banks started to understand incorrectness of this assumption, but to change it was not immediately possible due to time constraints – the banks needed to recover as soon as possible after the interest rate shock, and available resources – at that time all the calculations were done manually as personal computers were still not available at all working places.

With regard to *resource allocation* during this period, things did not change much: liquidity and funding was raised through different channels, when it was not enough – the measures on the asset side could be done. Nevertheless, banks learned that the interest rates are subject to changes, so the net interest income (NII) and net interest margin (NIM) was forecasted and planned.

Capital was still not considered as a scarce resource, which is why no tasks and functions relating to capital were executed yet.

The history described in this chapter helps to conclude that in the 1970s and 1980s the ALM tasks already were explicitly formulated, ALM area gained its importance and right to exist. The banking society had to overcome the ALM risk, in addition to a widened task of targeting balance sheet structure, as some new methods and instruments appeared (see Table 2.2). The ALM concept that was applied at that time can be called a concept of *minimum risk,* reflecting the changes in ALM tasks, methods and instruments.

Table 2.2: Minimum risk ALM concept (1973–1986).

1973–1986		**ALM risk management**	**BS structure targeting**	**Price benchmarking**	**Resources allocation**
Short-term/tactical tasks		Operational liquidity management Cash and equivalents management Interbank placements Exchange operations Cash flows analysis			
Long-term/ strategic tasks	**Going concern**	Interest rate risk management Interest rate gap modelling Liquidity risk management	Debt issuance Raising long-term funding Volumes planning Funding planning		NII and NIM forecasting

Chapter 3
Emergence of Derivatives

At the end of the 1980s some new shocks came and resulted in new conclusions, changing the way banks addressed their risks. First, the end of the 1980s was famous for savings and loan crises, which led to the proclaiming of insolvency of almost half of the savings and loan associations in the United States. Some reasons for the crisis lasted from the previously described period – rampant inflation, raising interest rates, and the recession in the early 1980s led to financial losses. Deregulation of the savings and loan industry introduced new risks and speculative opportunities, which were difficult to manage, combined with regulatory forbearance, allowing insolvent savings and loan associations to continue operating, as well as inner fraud worsening the situation and increasing defaults.

An example of savings and loan associations showed to the banks that not all the risks were properly eliminated. This gave banks the idea to start using derivatives for hedging. Banks concluded that if there were no available hedging instruments by means of balance sheet management, the risk was transferred to the area where those instruments existed. The fact that in January 1986 the British Bankers' Association (BAA) started calculation and quotation of the Libor rate, can be considered as a confirmation of emergence of derivatives in banking. Libor immediately gained popularity and became (until the latest period described in this book) the main indicator/reference rate for floating rate contracts, including floating legs of derivatives, all over the world in main currencies.

Another factor that also led banks to derivatives and other off-balance sheet instruments was new banking regulations in the form of Basel recommendations (now known as Basel I) introduced exactly at this time (in 1988). These short, in comparison to the current version, regulations (which fully came in force in 1992) tried to address and consider balance sheet credit risk, its impact on the capital adequacy and banks' sustainability. It emphasized an importance for regulators to take into account the IRR and investment risk on securities, but the document did not elaborate complicated models for its assessment and capturing in capital adequacy calculations. At the same time, Basel I noted, that it was needed to catch all off-balance-sheet activities within the capital adequacy framework, although there was limited experience in assessing risks of such activities, specific reporting systems were not implemented as the scale of such businesses was small – and thus, a simplified approach of converting into credit risk equivalents (by multiplying by credit conversion factors) was introduced. According to these details the regulators left opportunities for the banks to deal with off-balance-sheet instruments almost without constraints. This was the second major reason for bursting derivatives in banking during the late 1980s–1990s.

https://doi.org/10.1515/9783110669763-004

And so, banks, impacted by the sad experience of other financial institutions and the regulators' concerns about risks and sustainability, could not continue with the usual way of business and had to adjust their aims. The updated ALM aim was transferred into *managing risk off-balance*.

The new challenges required new ALM methods and instruments. Among the applied for asset and liability management instruments (including derivatives) during this period were the following:

- Interest rate futures
- Plain vanilla interest rate swaps (IRSs)
- Interest rate options
- FX forwards
- Credit default swaps (CDS)
- Financial innovations
- Securitization
- REPO operations
- Collateralized instruments
- Credit line facilities, loan commitments, letters of credit

The most popular and widely spread instruments were interest rate futures[1] and IRSs. Based on statistics as of 1993,[2] 92% of financial institutions applied IRSs for interest rate risk management of their loan portfolios. Figure 3.1 shows active development of the popularity of derivatives in the 1990s, which resulted in their massive expansion later.

This observation about new instruments is confirmed in theoretical papers of that time. For example, Katerina Simons[3] pointed out that although banks traditionally were managing the IRR only by closing interest rate gap (with balance sheet instruments), financial derivatives that appeared in the middle of 1980s became widely used by all the banks from the beginning of the 1990s.[4] The success of financial

1 "BIS Central Bank Survey of Foreign Exchange and Derivatives Market Activity," Bank for International Settlements, Monetary and Economic Department, May 1996; A.I. Brodt, "Optimal Bank Asset and Liability Management with Financial Futures," *Journal of Futures Markets* 8(4), 1988, 457–64.

2 K. Simons, "Interest Rate Derivatives and Asset Liability Management by Commercial Banks," *New England Economic Review*, Federal Reserve Bank of Boston. January/February 1995, 17–28; "BIS Central Bank Survey of Foreign Exchange and Derivatives Market Activity," Bank for International Settlements, Monetary and Economic Department, May 1996.

3 K. Simons, "Interest Rate Derivatives and Asset Liability Management by Commercial Banks," *New England Economic Review*, Federal Reserve Bank of Boston, January/February 1995, 17–28.

4 K. Simons, "Interest Rate Derivatives and Asset Liability Management by Commercial Banks," *New England Economic Review*, Federal Reserve Bank of Boston, January/February 1995, 17–28; "BIS Central Bank Survey of Foreign Exchange and Derivatives Market Activity," Bank for International Settlements, Monetary and Economic Department, May 1996.

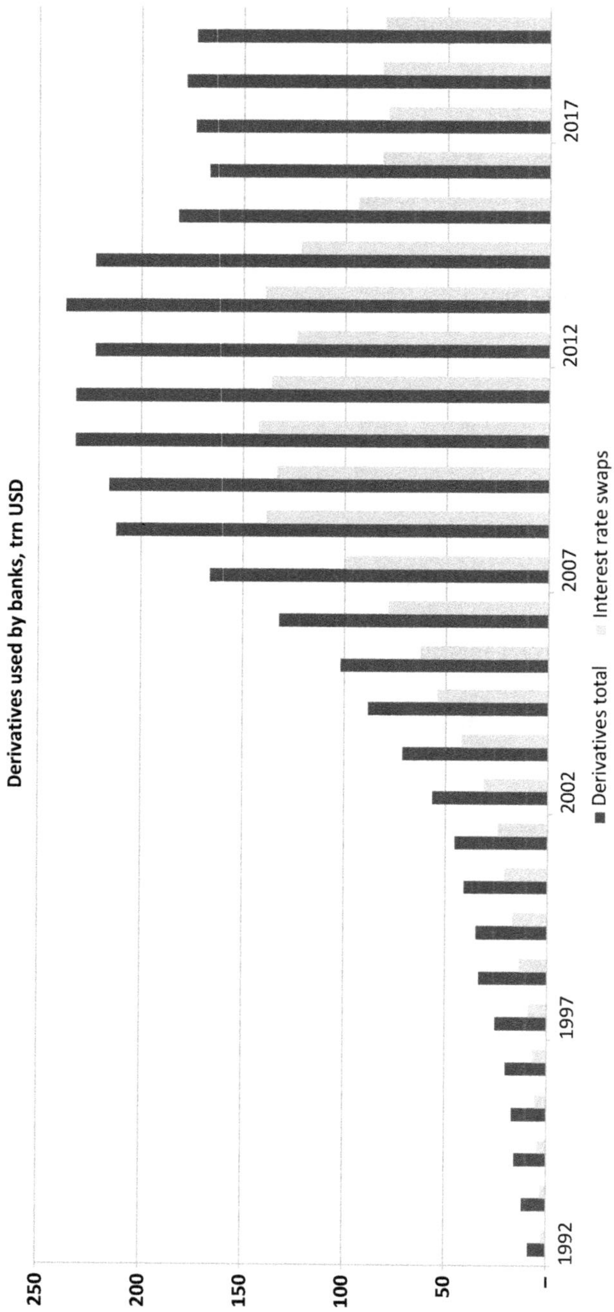

Figure 3.1: Derivatives used by banks, 1992–2019.
Source: Federal Deposits Insurance Corporation, Standard industry reports.

derivatives (high demand for financial institutions [in particular, commercial banks] for them for the execution of ALM) was explained by Simons as the "advantages of derivatives for risk management." She pointed out that derivatives were convenient, as they could change the balance sheet duration without additional consumption of capital for new products. From today's perspective it is clear that banks took advantage only by avoiding regulatory constraints through application of derivatives.

Box 3.1. Plain Vanilla IRS Mechanism

IRS is an important ALM tool, which is simply described in Figure 3.2. The most common application is for hedging IRR, which is described in Box 2.1.

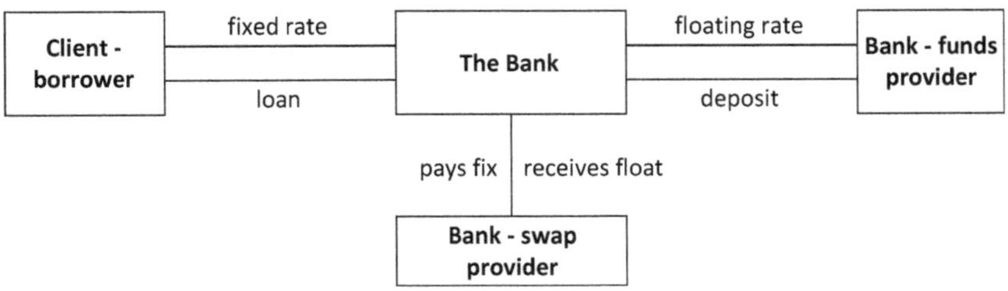

Figure 3.2: Plain vanilla IRS mechanism.

In a situation when a bank has granted a loan to a client at a fixed rate, but has funding at a floating rate, it is exposed to IRR, which will result, in the case of rising interest rates, in higher interest expenses and decrease in net interest margin. An IRS substitutes one type of interest payments by another; for example, banks pay a fixed rate for the swap and receive a floating rate in exchange. Amounts, of course, are neutralized with amounts of assets and liabilities, which are being hedged. The bank-swap provider, on contrary, will receive a fixed rate and pay a floating rate. This mechanism will help the commercial bank to equalize the timing of repricing of assets and liabilities and close the interest rate gap.

The rate payable on a swap represents the additional risk premium associated with counterparty's risk compared to money market rates. Before the 2007–2008 crisis, plain vanilla IRSs based on Libor were widely used for determining discount factors and implied forwards for IRS curve construction.

Many bankers and academic researchers (usually with a banking background) were very enthusiastic that ALM methods and approaches had shifted from boring gap analysis to real market deals, such as derivatives.[5] The explanations of derivatives' popularity varied from one working paper to another. In the early 1990s researchers

5 J.W. Bitner and R.A. Goddard, *Successful Bank Asset/Liability Management: A Guide to the Future Beyond Gap*. John Wiley & Sons, 1992.

assessed the dynamics of derivatives and made conclusions, for example by Elija Brewer and others,[6] about positive relations between derivatives and traditional balance sheet items (lending). It is worth noting, that this observation was correct only in the first years of using derivatives, although later their amounts skyrocketed and overtook any other balance sheet items' development.

Other academicians claimed profitability of derivatives as a major reason for their spreading all over the banking system. In the article by Edwards and Mishkin[7] the authors pay attention to a trend of de-regulation that was observed everywhere (in the United States, Europe, Japan) and led banks to losing their functions as intermediaries. Researchers notice that to stop profitability from dropping and to foster its recovery the banks started to widen their off-balance-sheet activities, which still were profitable.

Supranational organizations' working papers finally drew a link between accelerated growth of off-balance-sheet instruments, the lending of loans and profitability of banks, pointing out that one of the main reasons why non-loan-related activities have become so important for banks was because of higher risk weights for loans, than for other instruments, which put them at a comparative disadvantage in the profit-seeking strategies of banks.[8]

Regardless of the reasons that led to development of derivatives – it was already obvious that no ALM area of the bank was left unchanged during this period. In *ALM risk management,* two new approaches appeared. First, IRR management was executed through hedging with derivatives. The banks did not only raise funds with floating interest rates, but according to the decomposition of rates and tenors in their loan portfolios they also executed hedge deals with interest rate derivatives (e.g., with IRSs, substituting the floating rate cash flow of the liability by fixed rate cash flow of the derivative). At first the hedge accounting and revaluation mark-to-market was done by ALM teams themselves, because at this time the requirements were not demanding. FX rate risk was also naturally eliminated by hedging with FX forwards and futures. At that time bankers were not aware that risk could not be completely eliminated, but only transported from one to another (usually to credit risk). The regulators had not yet considered it properly in the requirements. That is why hedging with derivatives was considered as a panacea for all the banks.

As a second major change in *ALM risk management* a full new scope of activities connected with bonds was applied to liquidity risk management. The banks

6 E. Brewer, B. Minton, and J.T. Moser, "The Effect of Bank-Held Derivatives on Credit Accessibility," Proceedings, Federal Reserve Bank of Chicago 94(5), 208–28.

7 F.R. Edwards and F.S. Mishkin, "The Decline of Traditional Banking: Implications for Financial Stability and Regulatory Policy," NBER Working Paper, January 1995, No. 4993.

8 P. Slovik, "Systemically Important Banks and Capital Regulations Challenges Economics Department," *Organization for Economic Cooperation and Development* 916, OECD ECO/WKP (2011), 85.

started to form their bond portfolios that could be used for liquidity needs: as collaterals in REPO operations, which after mid 1980s got their new development, although in a more regulated way[9] (see Box 3.2) – and spread worldwide.

Box 3.2. Mechanism of Liquidity Improvement by Pledging Bonds with Central Banks
One of the sub-tasks of liquidity risk management is to ensure that a bank has sources of immediate liquidity improvement if needed. Central banks, acting always as lenders of last resort, elaborate special mechanisms and facilities, which serve the same aim. One such kind of facility is pledging of assets (in particular, bonds), which fulfill certain criteria within central banks. Of course, before a bank receives cash (cash loan) for the bonds, several steps should be executed (see Figure 3.3). ALM is the only responsible unit with direct communication with the central bank regarding collateralized assets.

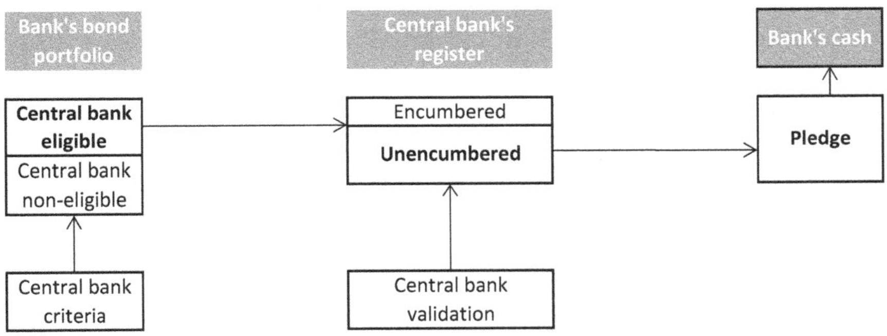

Figure 3.3: Mechanism of bonds pledging with central banks.

First of all, ALM should check eligibility criteria, what kind of assets/bonds satisfy the central bank in order to take them as collateral for a cash loan, and haircuts, which will be applied to bonds (amount of money provided for bonds is lower than the pledged amount). The eligibility criteria are published on central banks' web pages, together with the list of eligible marketable assets, which is updated daily. Usually there are requirements for type of asset (e.g., central government debt instruments, debt instruments issued by central banks, local and regional government debt instruments, supranational debt instruments, covered bank bonds, credit institutions' debt instruments, debt instruments issued by corporate and other issuers, asset-backed securities[10]), currency, place of issue and settlement, credit quality and acceptable markets.

Banks' ALM should monitor the criteria and flag the assets as eligible or not in its portfolio. Eligible bonds, if it is planned to pledge them, should be first transferred to the central bank's register on the

9 The REPO operations have always existed and were necessary for central banks' monetary policy execution, although several defaults with such instruments caused severe consequences in the market and made the regulators immediately address them. It is described in more details in Terry F. Rogers, The Government Securities Market: In the Wake of ESM, 27 *Santa Clara Law Review* 587 (1987).

10 See ECB eligibility criteria at: https://www.ecb.europa.eu/mopo/assets/standards/marketable/html/index.en.html

bank's securities account held with the central bank. ALM has at any point of time insight into its securities account, whereas the central bank records the information about unencumbered and encumbered assets of the bank. The validation of the portfolio held at the central bank's register is executed solely by the central bank, who applies haircuts and calculates the market value of the unencumbered portfolio. At the same time, ALM performs regular checks of the market value of the unencumbered portfolio based on the market information.

ALM can decide about pledging only if there are enough unencumbered assets with the central bank. If there are not enough, ALM instructs the back office to execute delivery of eligible assets to the central bank. Upon receipt of confirmation of unencumbered assets from the central bank, ALM decides on pledging and receiving cash.

Bonds as an instrument also could be observed for the *balance sheet structure targeting*. As it was written in the introduction to this ALM period – the regulatory requirements hardly considered off-balance-sheet exposures. Thus, the banks in order to free capital surplus started to use securitization: making pools of loans (e.g., mortgages) and issue bonds with collaterals of mortgage payment cash flows. This helped the banks to reduce off-balance exposure and expand their business further without any constraints.

Also it is worth mentioning, that as far as all on-balance assets received their risk weights for capital adequacy calculation – ALM started to take into account and plan the volumes of assets with different risk weights. Collateralized instruments were also used for targeting balance sheet structure, as, depending on the institution who issued the instrument to perform collateral, the risk weight could be significantly decreased and capital surplus freed. Credit risk equivalent of the off-balance-sheet exposure, as well as of interest rate/market risk was taken into account with application of credit conversion factors.

With these innovations ALM becomes more sophisticated and strategic. The balance sheet was planned for longer horizon, detailed funding and capital plans became an unattainable part of strategic planning and budgeting. Business lines and segments are compared between each other not only by such metrics, as return on assets (RoA), but also by return on risk weighted assets (RoRWA) with increasing understanding of the scarcity of capital as a resource. This is the first ALM task in area of *resources allocation* that appeared and has not changed as of today.

With regard to *price benchmarking and the FTP*, banks during this period tried to solve the problems of the past. First, the risk mitigation approach was substituted by multiple pool approach. It meant that the assets and liabilities were split in buckets within several tenors and one rate was assigned to each bucket. It was already a huge step forward and represented almost the current funds' transfer pricing system. Nevertheless, this simplified approach, of course, still had some drawbacks, as it did not give proper incentives for each tenor.

Also, lack of proper incentives is a reason for the second problem, which banks tried to solve. In the previous period, pricing was done on a non-prepayable basis, meaning that prepayment was not impacting the result of the business lines at all.

During this period banks already introduced "mark-to-market" prepayment penalty to business lines (so they could close the deal on the liability side if an asset was prepaid by a client). Although during this time interest rates declined and, thus, were accompanied by massive prepayments of fixed rate debt of all kinds. As a result, the profits of business lines were dominated by huge mark-to-market penalties. This caused a wave of misunderstanding and arguing. The only thing was obvious then: the pricing system failed to give the proper ex ante incentives to the business and needed to be updated.

The ALM history described in this chapter helps to conclude that in the 1980s to 1990s the scope of ALM tasks has significantly broadened, introducing plenty of new instruments and methods. ALM became a more strategical area for the bank improving mechanisms for ensuring banks' sustainability in the long run (see Table 3.1). The ALM concept, under which bank operated during this time, can be called the concept of "off-balance-sheet instruments," reflecting the changes in ALM tasks, methods, and instruments.

Table 3.1: Off-balance sheet instruments ALM concept (1986–1998).

1986–1998		**ALM risk management**	**BS structure targeting**	**Price benchmarking**	**Resources allocation**
Short-term/ tactical tasks		Operational liquidity management Cash and equivalents management Cash and equivalents management Interbank placements Repo operations Securities purchases Derivatives execution FX balances limiting Exchange operations	Capital measurement		
Long-term/ strategic tasks	Going concern	Interest rate risk management Interest rate gap modelling Liquidity risk management Balance sheet hedging	Debt issuance Raising long-term funding Securitization Funding and capital planning		NII and NIM forecasting RoRWA comparison
	Gone concern				

Chapter 4
Regulators in Place

The end of the 1990s to the beginning of the 2000s is famous for plenty of local financial crises, among which were the Asian financial crisis (1997), Russian financial crisis followed by the Long-Term Capital Management (LTCM) default (1998), economic crises in Latin America (1994–2002), and finally bursting of the dot-com bubble (2001). Although they were local and, thus, not impacting the whole world, their concentration from the aspect of time gave almost no chance to any of the large financial institutes to avoid the impacts of the crises. Even if the banks were not doing business with companies in the impacted countries, their balance sheets could contain debt issued by those countries or contracts with institutes who were heavily relying on emerging economies. The example of LTCM is very descriptive: the hedge fund had a strategy to explore arbitrage opportunities through investing in emerging markets' securities (including the Asian and Russian government debt) with high leverage by applying interest rate derivatives such as IRSs. When one of the derivative parts ("legs") defaulted – the whole scheme collapsed, exposing to realization of credit risk and losses all counterparties that were involved in the scheme. Moreover, even if there was no direct relation to the defaulting companies – the overall effect spread all over the market, impacting banks' balance sheets and profits and raising new questions and tasks for the regulators of the banking industry.

A lot of studies at this time were devoted to a topic on how to overcome consequences of these crises and what to do to avoid the repetition in the future. At this moment banks clearly understood that transferring of the risks off balance with the help of financial derivatives is not sufficient for efficient asset and liability management. Banks' balance sheets were still exposed to negative changes of the financial environment, which impact could be smoothed if banks were constrained by balance sheet regulatory limitations while allocating their resources to gain more profits (or maximization of capital).

During this time there was noticeable strengthening of banking activities regulations and limitations of banking risks by the supervisors. In particular, in 2001 the second edition of Basel recommendations was introduced at first for discussion[1] and then came into force in 2004 with an aim of full implementation by 2008. Its main difference from the Basel I was presentation of the three pillars split: the original pillar with setting capital requirements was enhanced by principles of supervisory review (the second pillar) and disclosure obligations (the third pillar). The first

1 Basel Committee on Banking Supervision, "Consultative Document. The New Basel Capital Accord." Bank for International Settlements, January 2001, issued for comment by 31 May 2001.

https://doi.org/10.1515/9783110669763-005

pillar (calculation and requirements for capital adequacy) was also amended by better operational risk and market risk quantifications based on data and formal techniques. The second pillar represented the first idea that regulators must perform their own review and impose institutions' specific requirements – further it would be more explicitly covered in the Committee of European Banking Supervisors (CEBS) guidelines on supervisory review process.[2] The third pillar (also known as "market discipline") aimed to complement the minimum capital requirements and supervisory review process by developing a set of disclosure requirements, which would allow the market participants to gauge the capital adequacy of an institution.

Supervisors also fully recognized that although capital had an important role to play in the mitigation (or, better to say, covering) of risks it may have not always been the sole or best solution. Regulators started targeting special treatment of some positions[3] that finally led to the split of the banking book and the trading book in banks, their instruments, limits and, as a consequence, risks.

The trend of the period was clear: banks were required to address with caution and even limit some of their activities, present a clear strategy of further sustainable growth and maintenance of sufficient profitability and capital. In line with this trend the ALM aim was also updated into *NII benchmarking within constraints*. It was obvious that for staying within the constraints banking units needed not only the theory how the requirements were calculated, but also a scenario analysis, what kind of activities and how – would impact the calculations. That is why ALM during that period became an intermediary between the business and risk management, equalizing the wishes of business and positions, which could potentially gain profits, together with the way risk management eliminates risk. ALM became an important unit within the bank with strategic view, which had the right to suggest adjustments and ideas to the bank's strategy from capital consumption/profit generation point of view. It was also emphasized in investigations of banking and finance professionals of those times.[4] All the developments in the banking world

2 Guidelines on the Application of the Supervisory Review Process under Pillar 2, CEBS, 25 January 2006.

3 The Application of Basel II to Trading Activities and the Treatment of Double Default Effects, BCBS, July 2005.

4 H.-W. Sinn, Risk Taking, "Limited Liability and the Competition of Bank Regulators," NBER Working Paper, December 2001, No. 8669; J.R. Barth, G. Caprio, Jr., and R. Levine "Banking Regulation and Supervision: What Works Best?" NBER Working Paper, November 2002, No. 9323; E.J. Kane, "Regulation and Supervision: An Ethical Perspective," NBER Working Paper, March 2008, No. 13895; L. Laeven, R. Levine, "Bank Governance, Regulation and Risk Taking," NBER Working Paper, June 2008, No. 14113; J.H. Van Bunsbergen, and M.W. Brandt, "Optimal Asset Allocation in Asset Liability Management," NBER Working Paper, March 2007, No. 12970.

mentioned in this chapter could be implemented in practice mainly due to the appearance of new ALM measures, instruments, and approaches:

- New risk quantification methods (value-at-risk [VaR] approach was preferred in Basel II for market risk; cash flow-at-risk [CfaR] and earnings-at-risk [EaR][5])
- Counterparty limits control
- Split of the banking book and the trading book (according to this logic, securities portfolio was split into the trading book portfolio used to receive trading speculative income and the banking book portfolio formed based on liquid securities with low level of credit risk in order to have a liquidity cushion, a reserve of funds, and to fulfill the liquidity regulatory requirements)
- FTP curve construction

ALM risk management was also enhanced at that time by new tasks. Split of books, aims, and risks within banking activities resulted in ALM full responsibility for banking book securities management. They were used to create a proper liquidity buffer for the bank; therefore, their characteristics were thoroughly investigated in order to provide reliability, good creditworthiness, eligibility to be used as collaterals and pledges. Regulatory guidelines on "Technical aspects of the management of interest rate risk arising from non-trading activities under the supervisory review process"[6] gave framework for proper banking book securities management.

With the new goal ALM also gained another dimension of the tasks: already usual interest rate and/or liquidity gaps started to be calculated in dynamics. Gap modelling/simulation became a new instrument in the area of *ALM risk management.*

Implications of this time were later analyzed in working papers and researchers that aimed to find the reason of the crisis in 2007. Some economic studies, including Andrea Beltratti, René M. Stulz,[7] emphasized, that banks with "more restrictions on their activities and stronger oversight of bank capital" before the crisis of 2007 were better performing also during the crisis. That means that importance of capital and own funds structure became for ALM in the beginning of 2000s higher than ever. Every single operation in the bank and the overall strategy of the bank had to be properly checked whether it negatively impacted the capital position or not.

---

5 For example, M. Carey and R.W. Stulz, "The Risks of Financial Institutions," NBER Working Paper, June 2005, No. 11442. CfaR and EaR were introduced by Rene Stulz in his book, *Risk Management and Derivatives*. Ohio: Thomson Southwestern, 2003. Cash flow-at-risk and earnings-at-risk approaches, in comparison to value-at-risk approach requiring all assets and liabilities included in the calculation to be liquid, assume that cash flows and earnings provide better assessment of banks' ability to finance its investments and payout liabilities.

6 Technical aspects of the management of IRR arising from non-trading activities under the supervisory review process, CEBS, 3 October 2006.

7 Andrea Beltratti and René M. Stulz, "Why Did Some Banks Perform Better During the Credit Crisis? A Cross-Country Study of the Impact of Governance and Regulation," NBER Working Paper 15180, July 2009.

Updates in *balance sheet structure targeting* were not limited only to such modelling. Introduced in Basel II the Internal Capital Adequacy Assessment Process (ICAAP) and then later issued the Capital requirements directive (there were different editions beginning on 1 January 2007) provided supervisors with several tools to steer the banks, including setting a Pillar 2 capital requirement, specific to a bank. ALM was forced to reconsider the own funds structure and to explore any possibilities to optimize it. For example, banks could optimize the capital structure by using up to its maximum level (in percentage to risk weighted assets) Tier II capital in form of subordinated loans and other obligations. This was important to provide better return on equity (RoE) and to be more attractive to investors and existing shareholders.

Further improvement of RoE also served *FTP* that during this time period developed significantly. First of all, matched maturity approach was elaborated and accepted as the best one to define the proper target for both sides of the balance sheet. Second, during these years personal computers at work allowed banks by trial-and-error iterations to calibrate an appropriate FTP curve for the bank. Banks immediately started to distinguish between market approach, cost approach, and mixed approach for the FTP curve construction.

Box 4.1. Development of FTP Curve Construction Methods

Methods of FTP curve construction developed gradually. First only "market," "cost," and "mixed" approaches appeared, only later with some regulatory guidance they were supplemented by "marginal" approaches.

In *"cost" approach* (based on the borrowing rates) FTP rates motivate placement of funds at a higher rate than the rate at which the funds were raised. This method could be applied on a calm market with low volatility of rates when the bank had a diversified liability structure with funds for different tenors and in order to give incentive to lending units to place money above the funding cost (when long-term expensive funds were previously raised).

In "cost" approach, an FTP rate is an average borrowing rate defined according to the current (or historic) contents of liabilities. It can be only one rate or several rates, calculated for different periods; it can be a moving average of historical interest rates on deposits with or without different weights (the elder observation will have a smaller weight, while most recent ones will have higher weights).

It was probably the easiest and most obvious approach to give incentives and targets about lending prices (with absolute objectivity and simplicity of calculation), although from current perspectives this method seems to have too many drawbacks:

- Dependence on the rates in the past, reaction on the market changes with a time lag
- The yield curve can be distorted because liabilities on different tenors can be raised at different times in the past
- When there are too many liabilities not placed into loans (on some tenors) this method does not provide an instrument for deposit volume regulation
- Does not allow steering of risk

In *"market" approach* (based on market interest rates) FTP rates reflect the rate of alternative placement of funds or borrowing in the market and change according to the markets dynamics. The applied market indicators should satisfy the following requirements:

- Properly in time they reflect the market situation
- Quotes are published in well-known sources and are available for all market participants (or calculated according to widely accepted formulas)
- Instruments can define the spread to the market indicator to get the level of the funding cost for the bank

Usually banks applied Libor (Euribor etc., later Eonia and Ester), IRS, cross-currency swap (CCS), and CDS as market indicators for FTP curve construction. When CDS was not available, bond yields as market quotes could be used. This approach was applied widely and for long term, as it possessed undeniable advantages:
- Objectivity and transparency (as a consequence, high level of trust)
- Instant reflection of the level of the market rates
- Possibility to define FTP rates even for those tenors at which no balance sheet items exist
- Construction of a smooth curve without distortions

However, there are also limitations of this method, which may have appeared to be the reason for developing and shifting preference to "marginal" approaches:
- Volatility of the money market indicators that is too high
- Lack of market indicators for middle term and long term on some markets
- Low volume of deals with government bonds on some markets and as a result loss of marketability of quotes
- Insufficient volume of deals and instruments for representativeness of the results for mathematical modeling

"Mixed" approach (based on the sum of the interest rate curves) takes into consideration diversified contents of liabilities at different tenors, which means it is a mixture of the market curve and the curve based on actual costs of liabilities.

The construction itself consists of three steps: (1) construction of the FTP curve based on market approach, (2) analysis of stable funding sources for each tenor and calculation of the weights of each type of liability in total liabilities of this time bucket, and (3) obtaining the weighted FTP curve by summing up of yield curves of different liabilities.

This method was applied by some banks due to, as they thought, many advantages:
- The current structure of liabilities and the costs of funding is considered
- Market component helps to reflect the fluctuations of market conjuncture
- Cost component helps to take the actual cost of funds into account

The disadvantages included time-consuming calculation and subjectivity when balance sheet lacked long-term liabilities. This method phased out together with the "market" approach.

"Marginal" approach appeared based on regulatory recommendations, "the transfer prices should reflect current market conditions as well as the actual institution-specific circumstances."[8] Putting it simply, that means the curve should contain a market component responsible for IRR and a bank-specific spread over the market, which will reflect the liquidity cost for the bank. "Marginal" approach relies on the price of the following additional asset or liability.

Attractiveness of this method is due to its advantages:
- Overall the curve reflects the market level of rates
- Reacts comparably fast on market changes
- Allows to set an FTP rate for those tenors for which no balance sheet liabilities exist

8 Guidelines on Liquidity Cost Benefit Allocation, CEBS, October 2010.

The fact that this method is considered the best one by the regulators does not mean that it lacks disadvantages. They are:
- Subjectivity of assessment
- Severe dependence of this method's adequacy on the depth of market of lending/borrowing instruments and the chosen instruments as benchmarks
- Possibility of distortions of the yield curve
- Limited opportunities to hedge interest rate risk

"Marginal lending" approach is less popular by bankers than the "marginal borrowing" approach. It is applied by small banks operating in rather developed local financial markets that can't rely on the liability side. For application of this method a deep and diversified market of lending instruments should exist.

A vast majority of banks apply *"marginal borrowing" approach*. For better performance of this approach, banks should have a diversified balance sheet structure. This requirement is due to the need to outline the core liabilities, which are:
- Funding sources where volumes are sensitive to interest rate changes – to ensure the possibility to regulate the inflow/outflow via changing the level of interest rates
- Funding volume is sufficiently high for banks' financing needs
- Overall structure of each funding source is stable

The steps to construct a curve using the "marginal borrowing" approach are as follows:
1. Selection of the relevant funding sources (core liabilities) for the bank:
   a. Analysis of all the sources of funding existing for the bank
   b. Assessment of the additional amount needed to be borrowed at the current moment
   c. If there's no need to raise funds at the moment, the rates are decreased to the level when no additional funds are raised
2. Gathering of information to obtain the rates:
   a. That could be actual quotes at what level the bank can raise funds (e.g., the rates for retail products published at the bank's website).
   b. In some cases, it can be an assumption of the business at what rate it is possible to borrow the required amount of funds.
3. Determining weights, which reflect the marginal funding mix. The weights can be derived either from the actual balance sheet structure or from the budgeted balance sheet structure for the future period and should reflect the possibilities of a bank to raise these kinds of funds.
4. Weighted rates on different tenors form the FTP curve, which can be used to determine rates for any tenor by means of internal interpolation.

The long-lasting problem of internal pricing – the prepayment cost – was finally solved during this period of time by incorporating the cost of a prepayment option (the embedded option in the product) in the funds transfer rates for particular deals. Pricing became more precise, as internal pricing models started to consider, at least for some products, also credit risk of the instruments, cost of capital, consumed by the instrument, and other expenses. Nevertheless, FTP stayed mainly for ex-post performance measurements, and ex-ante calculators for separate deals were still to come.

All these innovations in ALM and in banking overall led to increased awareness of bankers about risk and return drivers. This, in turn, was supposed to boost sustainability of the banking system worldwide, as, according to observations of analysts[9] of that time, there was a clear relationship between managers possessing bank-specific knowledge and skills and less risk taking.

It can be claimed that in the beginning of the 2000s ALM not only became a unit in banking, but a self-standing scientific area. The scope of its tasks, methods, and instruments (see Table 4.1) enlarged to such a scale that there could be separate approaches for large banks and small ones, for ones operating in developed markets and solutions for developing markets (for these differences see Part 3). What was definitely clear at that time is that this area should be ready for new challenges (and history showed that they would come), and in order to better meet them the homework on proper implementation of what already was announced and developed by supervisors and other banks should be done. The ALM concept of this period can be termed as *balance sheet restrictions*, reflecting the changes in banks' asset and liability management.

9 Luc Laeven and Ross Levine "Bank Governance, Regulation, and Risk Taking," NBER Working Paper 14113, June 2008.

Table 4.1: Balance sheet restrictions ALM concept (1998–2008).

1998–2008		ALM risk management	BS structure targeting	Price benchmarking	Resources allocation
Short-term/tactical tasks		Operational liquidity management Cash and equivalents management Interbank placements Repo operations Securities purchases Derivatives execution FX balances limiting Exchange operations Cash flows analysis Collateral management Counterparty limits control	Capital adequacy steering	FTP curve construction	
Long-term/strategic tasks	Going concern	Interest rate risk management Interest rate gap modeling Liquidity risk management Contingency planning Balance sheet hedging Determining metrics and limits	Debt issuance Raising long-term funding Securitization Funding and capital planning Defining capital structure	Product pricing Business profitability models Funds transfer pricing Maturity matching	NII and NIM forecasting Target RoE setting RoRWA comparison Strategy development RWA and capital allocation Cost of capital definition
	Gone concern	ILAAP execution	ICAAP execution		Economic capital calculation and allocation

Chapter 5
Preservation of Basel III Capital

As previously described, new challenges come together with turbulences, crises, and large defaults with domino effects. Of course, prior to the 2020 crisis, the widest negative event of the recent past was the "Lehman" crisis with its implications on financial industry worldwide. It started with the subprime mortgage crisis in the United States in 2007, and then was followed by the Lehman Brothers' investment bank that faced huge losses and collapsed after the Federal Reserve declined to guarantee its loans. By this time financial institutions worldwide were strongly interconnected – disappearance of one member in the chain led to severe disruptions of operations of the whole chain: Merrill Lynch went bankrupt and was purchased by Bank of America, the Federal Reserve took over the American International Group, Goldman Sachs and Morgan Stanley converted themselves from investment banks to bank holding companies to increase their protection by the Federal Reserve. There are detailed investigations on the causes of this crisis, although one cause was definitely clear: banks were making their profits through excessive risk-taking, and to avoid repeating such scale of crises the supervisors and banks together had to elaborate and develop preventing systems and processes.

First reply to the crisis was a publication by BCBS, "The Basel Committee's response to the financial crisis: Report to the G20."[1] It covered the areas to which changes should be introduced and proposals made on their enhancements. Among significant areas it was mentioned: (a) quality and level of regulatory capital; (b) liquidity management standards and supervision; (c) risk management and supervision including enhanced Pillar 2 guidelines; (d) enhanced Pillar 3 disclosures related to securitization, off-balance sheet exposures, and trading activities, which would promote transparency; and (e) cross-border supervisory cooperation. Separately were addressed problems of cyclicality and systemic importance. These topics were the basis for Basel III, which was introduced in 2012 for gradual implementation until 2019 (later some parts were postponed even further). After the introduction of Basel III the whole banking package was revised, imposing on banks new rules and requirements.

Additional regulatory requirements meant for the banks shortened the margin as they were aimed to curb risk that could (in plausible circumstances) lead to better profits. This effect was doubled due to low rate environment in developed financial markets. Banks had to find their way of business in the new environment, and

1 Basel Committee on Banking Supervision "The Basel Committee's Response to the Financial Crisis: Report to the G20," Bank for International Settlements, October 2010.

https://doi.org/10.1515/9783110669763-006

ALM, as usual, had to guide banks through. The new aim for ALM in this period can be formulated as *definition of prudent management buffers.* It means that in each banking area there should be an evaluation of possible risks (in various scenarios), their quantification in capital, liquidity and pricing terms, and drilling down as management guidelines. The business received some limitations within which they could operate, and at the same time the banks were secured against unpredictable shocks of the market that could significantly consume their resources. Again, with a new ALM task new methods and instruments were elaborated:

- Scenario analysis of all banking areas
- Various liquidity horizons
- Early warning and emergency indicators
- Hybrid instruments
- Additional Tier 1 capital issuance
- Internal capital and liquidity buffers justification
- Trading book/banking book management
- Internal ratings-based approaches for risk evaluation
- Recovery and resolution planning

ALM risk management area that was almost fully formed during previous periods has not changed a lot. To the already existing instruments and technics of risk management only a few new instruments were added for having risk assessment in even more dimensions (scenario analysis): not only in baseline "going concern" scenarios, but also in stressed "gone concern" conditions. Liquidity stress testing and even cash-flow stress testing became a part of banks' everyday life.

Furthermore, regulators strengthened the rules for separation of the banking book and the trading book activities. Immediately after the "Lehman" crisis several regulatory updates were implemented: they ranged from a prohibition of speculative activities (Volcker Rule), ring-fencing of systemic activities (proposal by the Vickers Commission), ring-fencing of risky activities (proposal by the Liikanen Group) to a full separation of commercial and investment banking (as under the Glass-Steagall Act). All proposals tried in some way or another to separate non-traditional, market-based activities from traditional banking, as taking deposits and granting loans. Basel committee introduced some more sophisticated measures: starting from 2012 Basel Committee has issued several papers on Fundamental review of the trading book in order to adapt existing rules of taking market risk into account in capital adequacy calculation as well as to prevent regulatory arbitrage by allocating positions to the trading book and the banking book. Key change was moving from VaR to expected shortfall (ES) and stressed ES.

Banking book securities management was also even more enhanced with two adjustments of original CEBS guidelines as of 2006. First, by the interest rate risk in the banking book (IRRBB) rules issued by the European Banking

Authority (EBA) in 2015,[2] where scenarios and stress testing were key elements even before measurement assumptions and governance of the IRR. Second, by Guidelines on the management of the IRR arising from non-trading book activities as of 2018.[3] The later guidelines addressed among other relevant points the overall IRRBB strategy and internal capital identification, calculation and allocation questions.

Concerning the *balance sheet structure targeting* issues, during this period there was continues arguing about levels of regulatory requirements and what constraints should be introduced to cover all possible risks (new requirements for capital, new liquidity measurement systems were often suggested even in academic papers[4]). The coefficients/requirements were imposed not on separate parts of the balance sheet but were developed as integrated measures and combination for different balance sheet/off-balance items. Liquidity measures were constructed using both sides of the balance sheets. For example, introduced in Basel III Liquidity Coverage Ratio (LCR) and Net Stable Funding Ratio (NSFR) include also a stressed-component, accounting the probability of inflows and outflows from different balance sheet/off-balance items during predefined time frames. As far as the ratios are subject to fluctuations (especially when large cash inflow or outflow occurs), it was particularly important to define safe internal buffers.

Box 5.1. Liquidity Buffer Planning for LCR

According to Basel III, LCR is a ratio resulting from dividing the amount of high-quality liquid assets (HQLA) in stressed conditions by the estimated stress scenario outflows over 30 days:

$$\frac{\textit{Stock of HQLA}}{\textit{Total net cash outflows over the next } 30 \textit{ calendar days}} \geq 100\%$$

HQLA constitute such liquid assets that can be immediately converted into cash at little or no loss of value, and usually are represented by central banks eligible for intraday liquidity needs and overnight liquidity facilities. HQLA, as a rule always actively traded and have a proven record as a reliable source of liquidity, are split into two groups. Level 1 assets are those of higher quality and are not subject to a haircut under the LCR. Level 1 includes only cash (coins and banknotes) and government securities, which (with few exceptions) have 0% risk weight for credit risk in capital adequacy calculations. Level 2 assets are of lower quality and should not constitute more than 40% of the overall HQLA after haircuts have been applied (15% haircut for Level 2A assets and 25%–50% haircut for Level 2B assets). Level 2A assets include government securities, which have

---

2 EBA/GL/2015/08 "Guidelines on the Management of Interest Rate Risk Arising from Non-Trading Activities, Final Report," EBA, 22 May 2015.

3 EBA/GL/2018/02 "Guidelines on the Management of Interest Rate Risk Arising from Non-Trading Book Activities," EBA, 19 July 2018.

4 For example, A. Krishnamurthy, J. Bai, and Ch.-H. Weymuller, "Measuring Liquidity Mismatch in the Banking Sector," NBER Working Paper 22729, October 2016.

20% risk weight for credit risk, and corporate securities/covered bonds, with high credit rating (a long-term credit rating from a recognized external credit assessment institution (ECAI) of at least AA or its equivalent). Level 2B assets can be included in LCR calculation at the discretion of national authorities and may include other types of securities.[5]

Net cash outflows are calculated as a difference between outflows and inflows (which are not higher than 75% of all outflows), weighted according to the probability of their occurrence (LCR factors).[6] For outflows these factors differ from 0%–5% for secured funding transactions and stable retail and SME deposits from 50%–100% for funding from legal entity customers and secured by non-HQLA funding transactions. For inflows, the LCR factors are decreasing from 50%–100% for lending transactions for different counterparties to 0%–15% for lending transactions backed by HQLA.

Table 5.1: Calculations of liquidity buffer for LCR.

Type of assets	**Amount**	**LCR factor**	**Inflow**
Central bank loan	5	100%	5
Corporate loans	20	50%	10
Total	**25**		**15**
Type of liabilities	**Amount**	**LCR factor**	**Outflow**
Central bank funding	10	0%	–
Other interbank funding	25	25%	6
Retail current accounts	20	10%	2
Retail term deposits >30 days	35	0%	–
Legal entities deposits	15	100%	15
Total	**105**		**23**
Liquidity buffer for LCR 110%	= 110%	* net outflow =	9

In a simple example in Table 5.1 t is shown how the necessary liquidity buffer amount can be calculated for a bank:

- As a first step, for different types of assets and liabilities the LCR factors are assigned, according to the LCR Basel III guidance.
- Then, the separate LCR inflows and outflows are calculated. In our example the LCR inflow equals to 15 and the LCR outflow equals to 23.
- As a next step, the total amount of outflows and inflows should be checked, if inflows do not exceed 75% of total outflows. If it exceeds, then as net outflows an amount of 25% of total outflows should be applied. In our example inflows do not exceed 75% of the outflows (the ratio is 65.2%). So the net outflow will be 23 – 15 = 8.
- Finally, liquidity buffer need (the amount of HQLA) is calculated by multiplication of subsequent LCR ratio (in the current example it is taken as 110%, as in reality liquidity shouldn't be steered at regulatory minimum, but with some buffer to it) and the net outflow. With the numbers of our example we will get 8 * 110% = 8.8.

5 In details they are described in LCR 30 "High-Quality Liquid Assets," BCBS, 15/12/2019.
6 Full list of LCR factors is presented in LCR 99 "Application Guidance," BCBS, 15/12/2019.

During this period all the risks were prescribed to be quantified in capital terms. At the same time, *capital management* became a separate and particularly important area for banks. With development of capital directives (CRD II in 2009, CRD III in 2010 with implementation time in 2011, CRD IV in 2013, which was valid for a rather long time), risks of economic cyclicality, systemic importance, and their impacts on capital were captured. That resulted in introduction and phase-in of capital buffers: capital conservation buffer, capital counter-cyclical buffer, systemic risk buffer, and its equivalents (see Box 12.1: Decomposition of Regulatory Capital Requirements). In addition to capital buffers, generally prescribed for all the banks (at least operating in the same country and being of the same size) there were updates on Pillar II in the form of allowance as a result of supervisory review and evaluation process (SREP) to impose individual quantitative capital requirements on banks in the form of Pillar II requirement and Pillar II guidance.[7] The latter one was defined as a result of the regulatory stress test of a bank based on EBA methodology. These add-ons could be introduced separately on different layers of capital (CET1, T1, and total capital) and resulted in a necessity always to compare surpluses of each capital level to regulatory requirements. This task contributed to development of various capital instruments. One example is additional tier 1 (AT1) capital that is usually reflected on the balance sheet as liability, although it has no maturity and can be converted into capital after some trigger event (according to CRR,[8] at the latest by CET1 reaching a level of 5.125%).

After Basel III introduction, the amount of AT1 capital increased abruptly and remains until now at a higher level (see Figure 5.1). Banks such as UBS, Société Générale, Credit Suisse, Deutsche Bank, and Royal Bank of Scotland issued about €91 billion of AT1 capital from April 2013 until early 2016.[9]

One more ratio observed by banks was leverage ratio. As regulators could imagine that through introduction of internal ratings-based approach banks could decrease risk weights and total RWA amount and, thus, show higher capital adequacy ratios – they introduced the leverage ratio to have one more constraint on capital. On the contrary to capital adequacy ratio, which relates own funds to risk weighted assets, leverage ratio observes the relation of own funds to total exposure, which includes on-balance sheet exposures, derivative exposures, securities financing transaction exposures, and off-balance sheet items.[10] By the time this book was finalized, leverage ratio still hadn't become binding: the 3% leverage

7 EBA/GL/2014/13 "Guidelines on Common Procedures and Methodologies for the Supervisory Review and Evaluation Process (SREP)," EBA, 19 December 2014 and EBA/GL/2016/10 "Final Report Guidelines on ICAAP and ILAAP Information Collected for SREP Purposes," EBA, 3 November 2016.

8 Article 54 CRR2.

9 E. Jeffery "AT1 Capital/CoCo Bonds: What You Should Know," Euromoney, July 15, 2019.

10 Leverage ratio, BCBS, 15.12.2019.

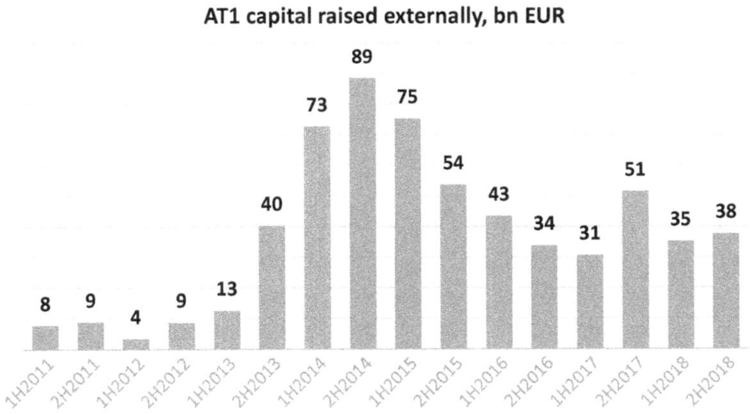

Figure 5.1: AT1 capital raised by banks, 2011–2018.
Source: BIS, Basel III Monitoring Report, October 2019.

ratio requirement will become binding on 28 June 2021 with coming in force of CRR II, but banks are already required to disclose their current leverage ratio (still being kept above its prescribed minimum of 3%). Since its first introduction in Basel III, total exposure calculation requirements for the purposes of the leverage ratio were updated for CRR II by introducing multiple exceptions, including the ones due to the COVID-19 pandemic.[11]

As far as there was almost always gradual implementation of regulatory capital buffers, the banks considered it plausible to have their own internal capital buffers. Later (closer to the end of this period) their importance was even emphasized by the regulators[12] and stated as necessary to fulfill them even in cases of stress.

As different stressed scenarios were of special concern by the regulators, it was not a surprise to learn that they wanted to also consider the banks' ease of recovery from crises of different severity and/or to understand possibilities to resolve the bank without significant harm to the market and financial system. With these regards banks had to define a system of early warning indicators, which would inform them and the supervisors that the bank must apply measures to return in a more stable stance. Early warning indicators represent capital, liquidity, and other risk buffers above minimum acceptable level (usually defined by the supervisor), which are lower than needed for usual going concern operating. In addition to early warning

11 https://www.bankingsupervision.europa.eu/press/pr/date/2020/html/ssm.pr200917~eaa01392ca.en.html

12 ECB Guide to the internal capital adequacy assessment process (ICAAP), EBA, November 2018 and ECB Guide to the internal liquidity adequacy assessment process (ILAAP), EBA, November 2018.

indicators each bank had to elaborate a recovery plan to show available options to restore capital and/or liquidity. Moreover, regulatory authorities also required from the banks explicit description of processes, systems, and interconnections between the bank and other counterparties – in order to resolve the bank in case of crisis within a very short time (the "resolution weekend") – on recovery and resolution planning see Box 14.1.

Vast regulatory coverage of banking activities also scrutinized the area of *price benchmarking*. With regard to the *FTP* – banks' attempts to construct an internal reference yield curve (either by using market bond quotes, or by using the bank's own balance sheet, or through other creative solutions) came to an end, when regulators starting from CEBS (currently EBA) in 2010 issued Guidelines[13] with a description of the rules for curve construction. It was once again confirmed that matched maturity approach should be used, and the appropriate way to construct the curve was based on marginal cost of funds. Here by marginal cost one should understand the price of raising an additional piece of funds through usual sources of the bank (either in the financial market, or through clients, or through other programs). Marginal cost can be applied to the marginal price of investing additional pieces of funds, but this method requires perfect financial markets and thus could not gain popularity.

Besides marginal approach in the regulatory guidance it was specifically emphasized that: the transfer prices should reflect market conditions (so that the rate would follow the market); internal prices should be aligned with wholesale market prices (and that would ensure that a large amount of funds can be raised through this source); adjustments to a base curve – the reference rate – should reflect the unique attributes of the financial institution (so to take into account the credit risk of the institution).

These changes had a natural impact on the pricing techniques: spread pricing when pricing of all new business was done at a spread above the marginal cost of matched maturity money (the reference rate). Moreover, understanding of the spread (or the net margin – the difference between the customer rate and the FTP rate) was at that time already available even at a stage of preparing the deal. Many ALM teams elaborated loan pricing calculators, implemented systems, which took actual FTP rates and with inputs of other parameters of the deal, such as expected credit risk, consumption of capital, provisions and operating expenses (e.g., for loans) – and gave the estimated net margin. Such ex-ante calculations helped banks to define appropriate levels of net margin ("buffers" above zero) and to avoid implausible deals.

---

13 Guidelines on Liquidity Cost Benefit Allocation, CEBS, October 2010. These Guidelines were followed by the Commission de Surveillance du Secteur Financier (CSSF), which published in 2012 a series of guidelines addressing central administration, internal governance, and risk management and also included a section on transfer pricing techniques.

One more development in the price benchmarking area was introduction and calculation of behavioral models, which allowed precise evaluation of the correspondent to such funds tenor – and then to use the marginal cost of the funds for determining the reference curve.

Changes in FTP led to new ideas and solutions in resource allocation. As an example, the reference FTP curve was used for managing the liquidity through regulation of the targeted pricing level: when there was excess of liquidity in a bank, the reference curve could be pulled down (the additional funding unit should be attracted only on a very low level, as there's no need for liquidity) – and the target for loan lending will be lower (or the business will be able to have more margin and, thus, would be more motivated). Or when a bank faces need for liquidity – it will have to curb lending, and this will be easily done by means of price benchmarking (higher FTP curve). It is also worth mentioning, that such benchmarking adjustments are available on any tenor and can encourage borrowing or lending at particular maturity to close liquidity and interest rate gaps, what makes an interlinkage with the ALM risk management area.

Not only was liquidity managed through the internal pricing mechanism, but also capital consumption could be influenced. As lending in different business areas (and definitely by subsidiaries in different countries) has to apply different risk weights to calculate capital adequacy ratios, one could speak about different capital consumption and subsequent costs of capital. If mortgages have lower risk weights (due to high collaterals) than corporate loans, the conclusion will be that a bank needs more capital to disburse the same amount of corporate loans, than for mortgages. Thus, the cost of capital (CoC) could and should be included in loan pricing, in order to ensure that margin (and profit) will be sufficient enough to build up consumed capital.

Incorporation of CoC into pricing did not get any regulatory guidance during that period of time, only an obvious general statement was announced that CoC should reflect the expected RoE of the bank/business lines/subsidiaries. Nevertheless, this interconnection of pricing mechanisms with future (estimated) profitability rose for ALM new tasks of RoE targeting (for separate business lines or for branches/subsidiaries), as well as NII and NIM forecasting through analysis and modelling of the balance sheet, with tenors and pricing.

As it can be seen (Table 5.2), the ALM developed into a large self-standing area, which connects almost all banking aspects within each other, controls that the bank acts in line with imposed by regulators limits and restrictions, stays in constant relation with supervising authorities on sustainability of the institution topics. The current set-up of ALM was formed almost all over the world, what is confirmed by BIS. According to BIS monitoring report, as of end-September 2019 all jurisdictions – members of Basel III implementation group already had risk-based capital rules, LCR regulations and capital conservation buffers in force. Almost all member jurisdictions also had final rules in force for the countercyclical capital buffer and systemic importance buffers, as well as issued final rules for the revised securitization framework.[14]

All external and internal buffers made it more complicated for banks to show high margins, in addition to low rates environment on a major part of financial markets. In order to reflect these changes and conclusions from them, the ALM concept of this period can be called concept of *low margin times,* implying all asset and liability instruments and measures to support banks even in such period.

14 Seventeenth progress report on adoption of the Basel regulatory framework, BIS, October 2019.

Table 5.2: Low margin times ALM concept (2009–2020).

2009–2020		ALM risk management	BS structure targeting	Price benchmarking	Resources allocation
Short-term /tactical tasks		Liquidity buffer management Operational liquidity management Cash and equivalents management Interbank placements Repo operations Securities purchases Derivatives execution FX balances limiting Exchange operations Cash flows analysis Collateral management Counterparty limits control	Capital adequacy steering	FTP curve construction	Liquidity cost calculation
Long-term/ strategic tasks	Going concern	Interest rate risk management Interest rate gap modelling Liquidity risk management Contingency planning Balance sheet hedging Determining metrics and limits	Debt issuance Raising long-term funding Securitization Funding and capital planning Defining capital structure	Product pricing Business profitability models Funds transfer pricing Behavioral modelling Maturity matching	NII and NIM forecasting Target RoE setting RoRWA comparison Strategy development RWA and capital allocation Cost of capital definition
	Gone concern	ILAAP execution Liquidity stress testing Cash flow stress testing	ICAAP execution Capital stress testing MREL forecasting Resolution planning Recovery planning		Economic capital calculation and allocation

Chapter 6
Complete Interrelation

While writing this chapter, this period had not yet started. Although, there is always some understanding, what should still be changed/updated. Moreover, authorities always give (a) time for consultation with banks – whether suggested requirements do not have unnoticed negative implications (as a result, regulators may even suggest amendments to methodology) and (b) transition periods – some time for preparation for upcoming regulatory updates, when banks may analyze the gaps and elaborate action plans, how within transition periods to update their balance and off-balance structures, IT infrastructure, and overall awareness. Detailed characteristics of this period are presented in Part 3 of the book, whereas below only the most important trends are outlined.

The beginning of this new period was predefined as a starting year of a new banking package – set of regulatory updates for banks, including Basel IV, CRR II, CRD V, and BRRD II, – which should have been fully implemented by 2021. The COVID-19 crisis impacted all the areas of life, and banking as well. Some of the planned changes were preloaded already in 2020, while some new regulations were postponed further. The important updates, which will define the new ALM period in a bank among others, include the following:
- Revised banking and trading book boundary and IRR management
- Libor transition and financial benchmark regulation review
- Recalibration of credit risk models (indirect effects of non-banking risks [like climate change or worldwide pandemics] should be considered)
- Better risk segmentation (systemic and countercyclical risks) and large exposure management
- Liquidity management outside predefined ratios ("cliff effect" mitigation)
- Financial interconnections management

What can be observed and concluded right now is that financial stability is a major concern of the regulators and banks, as never before. Banks and supervisors learned many lessons – starting from impacts of negative unpredictable one-offs on profit and loss (P&L) and RoE, and continuing with suspicious, larger than average, development (growth) of some portfolios that should require special treatment. The trends now are to reach better interrelations between all areas in the bank, to exclude regulatory arbitrage, to ensure for regulators that impact in one area is assessed throughout the bank and won't be missed.

Regulators raise importance to also incorporate economic effects of deals and economic risks across the bank, widening for ALM zones of responsibility and variety of indicators under its control. Now ALM has to first define the most binding indicator based on all available measures and instruments – "the bottleneck" and

https://doi.org/10.1515/9783110669763-007

then to cure it while the bank conducts different operations. Consequently, ALM priority task is now *solving multi-parametric optimization task.*

At this time ALM starts to play a central role in coordination and execution of impact assessments. As a reply to regulatory challenges, banks realized that if they separately tried to maintain liquidity ratios, heal the IRR, and fulfill capital requirements – all in all it costs too much and their profitability was not enough to continue the business. Nowadays hybrid instruments are developed and valued by the banking society, and finance professionals should possess not only a deep subject knowledge, but also a holistic view on the bank, understand all interconnections, and be able to find a combination of methods and instruments that would serve to take care of different ALM aspects.

All ALM areas are now closed in and interconnected. *ALM risk management* area is being enhanced by shifting its attention behind the horizons of the regulatory predefined ratios. From one side liquidity "cliff effects" should be avoided at any time (like the one right after the LCR[1] and before the NSFR). This requires proper planning of sustainable funding supply. From another side, liquidity instruments should be chosen to satisfy not only liquidity ratios, but also requirements toward overall balance sheet structure and types of liabilities and own funds (used, e.g., in minimum requirement for own funds and eligible liabilities [MREL] calculation). This is already a task for the *balance sheet structure targeting*, which also deals with targeting assets/portfolios with lower risk (systemic/concentration/countercyclical) to capital and lower losses in various potential stress tests. Thus, normative (regulatory) and economic perspectives in IRRBB, capital, and liquidity in baseline and adverse scenarios are showing even further interconnectedness.

Box 6.1. Introduction of the NSFR Requirement

NSFR has been introduced to banks already for some time, but still not fully phased-in and obligatory. First suggested by the Basel Committee in December 2010 it was supposed to be put in place by 2018. Although its effective date was further shifted to 28.06.2021, representing a part of the new Banking Package.

In comparison to LCR, which promotes the short-term resilience of a bank's liquidity risk profile by ensuring that it has sufficient HQLA to survive a significant stress scenario lasting for one month, NSFR has a time horizon of one year and requires that banks maintain a stable funding profile in relation to the composition of their assets and off-balance-sheet activities. The Basel standard on NSFR was published in October 2014.

NSFR is calculated according to a formula: $\frac{\textit{Available amount of Stable Funding}}{\textit{Required amount of Stable Funding}} \geq 100\%$, where assets and liabilities are assigned to available stable funding (ASF) and required stable funding (RSF) based on the probability of their outflow with a predefined in the methodology outflow factors. ASF represents the portion of capital and liabilities of a bank expected to be reliable over the one-year time horizon considered by the NSFR. The RSF is a function of the liquidity characteristics

1 Sensitivity Analysis of Liquidity Risk – Stress Test 2019 Final Results, ECB, 7 October 2019.

and residual maturities of various assets held by the bank as well as those of its off-balance sheet exposures.[2] The approximate distribution of ASF and RSF weights for different types of assets and liabilities is summarized in Figure 6.1.

Liability transformation	ASF weight	Asset transformation	RSF weight
Customer deposits		Cash	0%
Current	90%	Placements in Central Banks	
Saving	95%		
Term		Government securities	
Interbank deposits Short-term borrowing (<6M)	0%	Interbank loans (<6M)	10%
Long-term borrowing (>1Y)	100%	Interbank loans (6M-1Y) Corporate debt securities	50%
Other borrowing (6M-1Y)	50%	Unencumbered loans (>1Y)	85%
Capital	100%	Encumbered >1Y assets	100%

Figure 6.1: NSFR calculation weights for assets and liabilities.

While heading toward the phase-in of the NSFR, it is important for a bank to execute preparatory measures:
- Calculate several times NSFR and assess its volatility, using the most recent data (at least on a yearly basis using 2–3 data sets)
- Based on the volatility assessment, discuss at ALCO and approve internal limits for gradual increase of NSFR internal limit to enhance its smooth fulfillment without hindering the business
- Include in long-term funding plans gradual step-in of the internal NSFR until its final level

The targeting of particular instruments, assets, and liabilities can't be imagined without effects on pricing. *Price benchmarking* impacts decomposition of the balance sheet and *Resource allocation*. One such example is CoC component, which is a loan pricing element, but it also serves the purpose of proper allocation of resources (capital, in this case) to business lines and segments. Once again it is evident that short-term tasks should be in line with the overall strategy of the bank, and no space is left for any operations "by chance."

The impacts should be observed from different angles, and this evaluation results in determining the "bottleneck" – the most binding restriction. The "bottlenecks" can be pointed out in general: what is more scarce for the bank – liquidity or capital; or maybe introduced in detailed areas – normative or economic perspective for capital, which layer of capital is the scarcest, in baseline or stressed conditions? After

2 NSF 20 "Calculation and Reporting," BCBS, 15/12/2019.

determining the "bottleneck", banks have to find their own instruments focusing on maintaining this "bottleneck" and execute prudent governance.

With regard to many constraints and ability of banks to find solutions, there are arguments that banking regulations based on the Basel accords encourage unconventional business practices and contribute to adverse systemic shocks. According to the Organization for Economic Cooperation and Development (OECD) study,[3] capital regulation based on risk-weighted assets encourages innovation designed to circumvent regulatory requirements and shifts banks' focus away from their core economic functions. Tighter capital requirements may further contribute to these skewed incentives. New liquidity regulation, notwithstanding its good intentions, is another likely candidate to increase bank incentives to exploit regulation. ALM via its methods and instruments also must address this problem. Thus, its role as an intermediary between regulatory restrictions and the business profitability gains paramount importance. During this period the main characteristic of the ALM is that it becomes individual for each bank, and the name of the concept can be *overcoming bottlenecks*. In greater detail the ALM future projections are described in Part 3 of this book.

3 Patrick Slovik, "Systemically Important Banks and Capital Regulations Challenges," ECO/WKP (2011)85, Organization for Economic Cooperation and Development, Economics Department, Working Paper No. 916.

Chapter 7
ALM Evolution Summary

It is now clear that over time ALM tasks in banks have been changing. Before the 1970s there were controls over resource allocation, aiming to obtain a stable interest margin. With abrupt and unexpected growth of interest rates and, as a result, realization of IRR and liquidity risk in the second half of the 1970s, the main ALM task became minimization of financial risks by the closing of all possible open positions (gaps). With interest margin decrease at the end of the 1980s, ALM tasks were again modified: ALM teams were aiming to manage risk off-balance, as some regulatory gaps made it possible not to use capital surplus for that. New financial turbulence around the 2000s led again to a change of the main ALM task, which became net interest income benchmarking within regulatory constraints, as new restrictions tended to appear. Financial crisis in 2007–2009 also resulted in a new ALM priority task: definition and setting of prudent buffers to prevent repetition of the crisis and complying with regulatory updates. As open issues still impacting financial stability were taken into consideration, a new banking package was prepared to come into force. ALM again faced adjustments to its major task, which transformed into solving multi-parametric optimization tasks.

Changes to ALM tasks led to a development of new methods and instruments for asset and liability management in banks. These instruments and methods can be classified according to the ALM tasks for which they were applied. This classification is useful to understand when and why an instrument, or a method appeared and was applied.

Before the task to minimize risks appeared, there were not a lot of ALM methods and instruments, they did not change over time, and no new developments were needed. And although the method of interest rate spread fixing, which was used while structuring product lines for securing a stable interest rate margin for the bank, appeared before “the ALM era” it is still included in the first group of ALM methods and instruments, as it was used for the same purposes.

1) For closing the gaps (financial risks minimization) *balance sheet methods and instruments* for ALM appeared. They included:
    a. Asset volume planning (amount in loans and amount in liquid funds)
    b. Rollover of loans at new market rates
    c. Introduction of floating interest rates in contracts
    d. Selling of loan portfolios at the secondary market
    e. Individual programs for deposit raising
    f. Long-term debt issuance
    g. Gap management, including interest rate gap analysis, cash flow analysis, maturity matching, and immunization

https://doi.org/10.1515/9783110669763-008

2) In order to manage risk off-balance (without much consumption of capital) *off-balance sheet ALM methods and instruments* appeared. They consisted of:
   a. Hedging with derivatives:
      i. Interest rate derivatives (futures, options, plain vanilla IRSs)
      ii. FX derivatives (forwards, options, futures)
      iii. CDSs
   b. Financial innovations
   c. Securitization (with different loan pools – mortgage, leasing, etc.)
   d. Building up bond portfolios and REPO operations
   e. Collateralized instruments
   f. Credit line facilities, loan commitments, and letters of credit
   g. Insurance certificates against interest rate fluctuations
3) The next group of ALM instruments needed for NII benchmarking within constraints can be called *instruments and methods for sustainability maintenance.* They included all balance sheet methods and instruments, which helped to comply with regulatory limits:
   a. Banking book securities management
   b. Counterparty limits control
   c. FTP curve construction
   d. Interest rate gap modelling, quantification of market risk by means of VaR, CfaR, and EaR
   e. Determining of own funds structure, subordinated loans application
4) One of the reasons for the 2008–2009 crisis is a mismatch between cash flows and product flows (cash flows created by derivatives and other off-balance items exceeded the product flow multiple times). This led to a need of more thorough control over liquidity and impacts in various scenarios. As a consequence, ALM *multi-dimensional methods and instruments* appeared for prudent buffers definition:
   a. Scenario analysis and modelling of all areas (with different assumptions, varying liquidity horizons, behavioral patterns, etc.)
   b. Stress testing (of capital, liquidity, cash flow, ES)
   c. Balance sheet planning within regulatory requirements (LCR, NSFR, combined buffer requirements, leverage ratio, Pillar 2 capital requirements and guidance, early warning and emergency indicators)
   d. Internal buffers definition
   e. Hybrid instruments, incl. AT1 issuances for capital needs
   f. CoC incorporation in pricing
   g. FTP for ex-ante pricing, ex-post assessment, and liquidity allocation and management
5) *Interconnected (informing) methods and instruments* for ALM should be used to fulfill the new ALM task that appeared recently: solving multi-parametric optimization task. The new methods and instruments are applied to one area but

advise about possible implications on another banking area. Moreover, they are planned to solve issues between the areas or at their interception.

It is worth mentioning that tasks, methods, and instruments altogether constitute a concept. Thus, when tasks, methods, and applied instruments change, one can speak about change of a concept. The above classification leads to a conclusion that we have observed several times changes over the last century of an asset and liability management concept. Periodization of the ALM concepts is presented in a separate table (see Table 7.1).

1) Concept of "minimal intervention."
   Before the middle of the 1970s asset and liability management almost did not exist (only duration method was elaborated and applied since the early 1950s). For maintaining a stable interest margin level no complicated asset and liability methods were required. Thus, it can be concluded that from 1950 till 1973 the first ALM concept dominated, which can be called a "minimal intervention" concept.
2) Concept of "minimum risk."
   Change of the "minimal intervention" concept happened in the beginning of the 1970s as a result of markets' volatility increase and banks' acknowledgment of their risks. As a result, from 1973 until new turbulence banks started to use instruments for asset and liability management from the first group of the classification above: balance sheet methods and instruments. This group of ALM methods and instruments helped the banks to solve gap closings/risk minimization task. That is why it is logical to call the ALM concept for banks during 1973–1986 a "minimum risk" concept.
3) Concept of "off-balance-sheet instruments."
   Starting from the middle of the 1980s "minimum risk" concept was followed by the next concept, which contained off-balance methods and instruments (the second group of classification). Increased popularity of hedging with financial derivatives and securitization can be explained by the fact that banks could secure their balances against adverse external factors (against diverse financial risks) by means of transferring these risks off balance (and not consuming their capital in a way it could be with balance-sheet instruments). It also enabled banks not to create additional provisions, which decreased banks' own funds. Thus, approximately from 1986 until 1998 the "off-balance-sheet instruments" concept gained its actuality.
4) Concept of "balance sheet restrictions."
   With the end of the 1990s, priorities of banks in ALM shifted again. Banks needed to provide benchmark to the NII, having certain constraints. As a result, balance sheet methods and instruments for maintaining banks' sustainability appeared and established a new ALM concept. The main peculiarity of this concept is that applicability of already existing balance sheet methods and instruments was limited by specific ratios imposed by the regulatory authorities on

banking balance sheet items. These ratios were aimed to defend banks' balance sheets from negative impacts on NII and new instruments were helping in this task. The ALM concept for the 1998–2008 time period was named a "balance sheet restrictions" concept.

5) "Low margin times" ALM concept.
   2009–2010 showed that the "balance sheet restrictions" concept applied during that period was not efficient at all times. The main reason for this inefficiency is that some financial risk not yet eliminated by banks still applying usual ALM methods, was not treated prudently. The financial crisis emphasized a new ALM task to be solved by commercial banks: definition of prudent buffers. This task could be solved by assessment of less obvious risks and by application of buffers to regulatory requirements for possible realization of such scenarios that have never been experienced in the past. Banks had yet again to amend or adjust ALM methods and instruments in order to adapt themselves to the new requirements and to the new ALM concept, which is called a "low margin times" ALM concept. This concept can be observed in banks until the end of the 2010s when regulators introduced a new regulatory package addressing the necessity of constant interaction and interrelation between all the processes in banks and overall management steering. This widened the scope of topics and constraints, which should be taken into account by ALM.
6) "Overcoming bottenecks" ALM concept.
   As regulators continuously develop a methodological base for supervising banks and further ensure financial stability of financial systems, they emphasize in their recommendations to banks that all the processes should be interconnected and should inform each other. That is why no function can be sufficient without considering developments of other functions in a bank. It also relates to asset and liability management. The main ALM task since 2020–2021 transforms into incorporating impacts of all banking processes and restrictions on them into the holistic picture. Solving this task means for banks not only steering within the limits on assets, liabilities and off-balance items, but also process-wise and resource-wise managing the balance sheet. The new concept that is called an "overcoming bottleneck" ALM concept reflects a regulatory new package that is meant to come in force at this moment in time. Taking into account the average duration of the, so-called, ALM cycles (which also could be explained by the medium-term cyclicality theory which can be applied also to banks' balance sheets development) and also the phase-in period for new regulatory changes, this concept will be prevailing in banks for additional 8–10 years.

Even analyzing the concepts, it can be clearly seen that ALM went a long way from minimal intervention to overcoming bottlenecks in highly interrelated environments that once again points out the ever-increasing role of ALM in a commercial bank.

Table 7.1: ALM concepts evolution.

Period	**1950–1973**	**1973–1986**	**1986–1998**	**1998–2008**	**2009–2020**	**2020–20XX**
Name of period	*Before the ALM era*	*Financial turbulence*	*Emergence of derivatives*	*Regulators in place*	*Preservation of Basel III capital*	*Complete interrelation*
Name of ALM concept	***Minimum intervention***	***Minimum risk***	***Off-balance-sheet instruments***	***Balance sheet restrictions***	***Low margin times***	***Overcoming bottlenecks***
Reason to appear		Raising of interest rates as a result of oil crisis, collapse of Bretton Woods System, and start of Great Inflation in 1971–1973	Developing of derivatives, saving associations crises, composition of Basel I recommendations	Local defaults and crises in 1997–1998	Lehman Brothers crisis in 2007–2009, Basel III coming in place	Basel IV, CRR II, CRD V, BRRD II coming in place, COVID-19 crisis
ALM aim	Stable margin	Close the gaps	Manage risk off-balance	NII benchmarking within constraints	Prudent buffers definition	Solving multi-parametric optimization task
Measures and instruments	– Duration analysis	– Loan volumes planning – Old loans rollover at market rates – Selling of loan portfolios at the secondary market	– Interest rate futures, options – Plain vanilla interest rate swaps – FX forwards – Credit default swaps	– Split of banking book and trading book – FTP curve construction – Counterparty limits control	– Scenario analysis of all areas – Varying liquidity horizons – Early warning and emergency indicators	– Revised banking and trading book boundary – Recalibration of credit risk models for indirect effects of nonbanking risks

	– Flexible deposits at floating rates – Individual programs for deposit raising	– Financial innovations – Securitization – REPO operations – Collateralized instruments – Credit line facilities, loan commitments, letters of credit		– Hybrid instruments – AT1 issuance – Internal buffers definition – Trading book/ banking book boundary – Internal models-based approaches	– countercyclical/ concentration risk segmentation – Large exposure limitation – Financial interconnections management

(continued)

Table 7.1 (continued)

Period		**1950–1973**	**1973–1986**	**1986–1998**	**1998–2008**	**2009–2020**	**2020–20XX**
Approaches	**ALM risk management**	Liquidity gap analysis	Interest rate gap analysis Cash flows analysis Maturity matching	Hedging with derivatives Building up bond portfolios	Banking book securities management Interest rate gap modelling Value-at-risk (VaR) approach for market risk quantification Cash flow-at-risk (CfaR) Earnings-at-risk (EaR)	Expected shortfall (ES), stressed ES Cash flow stress testing Liquidity stress testing	Liquidity management outside predefined ratios ("cliff effect" mitigation)
	BS structure targeting		Targeting of portfolio durations through rollovers, prepayments, selling of portfolios, long-term debt issuance, individual deposit raising programs	Risk-weighted approach, RoRWA Credit conversion factors	Internal Capital Adequacy Assessment Process (ICAAP) Determining of own funds structure Subordinated loans raising	Balance sheet planning within regulatory requirements (LCR, NSFR, combined buffer requirements, leverage ratio, Pillar 2 Capital Requirements and Guidance – P2R and P2G) Capital stress testing	Business planning with accounting of the economic perspective Economic value of equity assessment and control MREL targeting

Price benchmarking and FTP	Single pool approach	Fixed/floating rates products Risk mitigation approach	Multiple-pool approach Start quotation of Libor	Matched maturity approach: – Market approach – Cost approach – Mixed approach	Marginal matched maturity approach, "spread pricing", behavioral modelling	Libor transition and financial benchmarks regulation review
Resource allocation		"Non-prepayable" basis: prepayments were not priced	"Non-prepayable" basis: ex-post penalties for prepayments	"Costless prepayment" through incorporation of the cost of a prepayment option in transfer prices FTP mainly for ex-post performance measurement	Targeting RoE, NII, NIM forecasting Cost of capital incorporation FTP for liquidity allocation and management (as an ex-ante mechanism) FRTB implementation	Addressing the "bottleneck" requirements

Conclusions

This chapter covered such topics as development of ALM tasks over time, classification of ALM methods and instruments, reasons for changes in ALM, and interconnection between ALM concepts.

Based on the observation that banks had to change their priorities in asset and liability management in different time periods, the ALM methods and instruments were systemized and classified the following way:

1) In order to minimize financial risks, balance sheet methods and instruments appeared
2) For managing risk off-balance – subsequent off-balance-sheet methods and instruments came into practice
3) Aim of NII benchmarking within constraints developed methods and instruments for maintaining banks' sustainability
4) For prudent buffers definition multi-dimensional methods and instruments started to be applied
5) For solving multi-parametric optimization tasks new – interconnected and informing – methods and instruments are required

This classification was used to construct overview and periodization of ALM concepts:

- 1950–1973 – "minimal intervention" concept
- 1973–1986 – "minimum risk" concept
- 1986–1998 – "off-balance-sheet instruments" concept
- 1998–2008 – "balance sheet restrictions" concept
- 2009–2020 – "low margin times" ALM concept
- 2020–2030s – "overcoming bottlenecks" ALM concept

https://doi.org/10.1515/9783110669763-009

Part 2: **Place of Asset and Liability Management in a Bank**

When anyone outside the banking industry imagines a bank, one thinks about loans and deposits and other services for customers that we became familiar with receiving from banks. When a bank is considered as an organization in general, then it's correct to speak about its organizational structure, with different departments, headed by the board of directors (the management board). The management board defines targets and goals for the bank and splits roles and responsibilities within the bank in a way that would ensure that a bank achieves the targets, provides proper and reliable services to customers, and does not impose risks to the financial system. But where inside the responsibilities split and among the products and services steering are the asset and liability management tasks?

This part answers the following questions:
- How does ALM address the goals of the management board?
- What kinds of ALM operating models exist?
- What are other departments that deal with the balance sheet risk management and how are their responsibilities split with the ALM?
- How does ALM avoid conflicts of interest while fulfilling its responsibilities?
- What are the differences between ALM desk in a stand-alone bank and a Group Treasury?

Multiple crises, which have recently occurred, showed that in different times the importance of management boards' responsibilities for a bank also differs. The usual responsibilities for the board are definition of a strategy, setting up proper governance, ethics and conduct, fulfilment of regulatory and wider stakeholders' obligations. However, starting from the crisis of 2008 (the Lehman's crisis) the list of usual responsibilities was enhanced by the governance of the balance sheet. Moreover, the crisis demonstrated in different jurisdictions in both large banking groups and small banks, that the proper balance sheet management is *primus inter pares* amongst the list of board responsibilities. The operating model for governance of balance sheet and ALM risk over the economic cycle since then becomes paramount. Through many years of development, ALM has become a real guardian of the balance sheet and off-balance items, its operating model, its place in the bank, and interrelation with other departments is also of paramount importance.

https://doi.org/10.1515/9783110669763-010

Chapter 8
Prerequisites for ALM

As was shown in Part 1, as soon as there are separate assets and liabilities in a bank, one can speak about asset and liability management. Of course, there should be possibilities to see/to retrieve characteristics of those assets and liabilities and off-balance items for their proper analysis and steering. This is usually solved by data warehouses in banks, by core banking systems, controlling cubes and various specific IT solutions. They will be different for large and small banks (see Chapter 14.1), but they will in any case provide the basis for the ALM.

Another question is how to understand what should be done with the balance sheet, so it satisfies the goals of the bank. Of course, there are always regulatory requirements, which by no means can be breached. But as it was emphasized in Part 1, there should be internal buffers defined, which serve to steer banks with a certain surplus to the regulatory minimum. These internal indicators are set in the RAS and the bank's risk appetite framework.

The RAS is an articulated explicit statement of board appetite for and tolerance of balance sheet risk, which incorporates qualitative and quantitative metrics and limits on banks' operations in each area. Along with strategy, RAS is one of the most important documents the board must sign off on. RAS constitutes the basis for the target risk profile and is defined as the bank's willingness to take on risks as quantified by the appropriate measures. For each of the measures identified, an overall bank-wide "macro-tolerance" is set, which is then, when appropriate, broken down into tolerances for individual business lines. The list of relevant measures and indicators, their assessment methodology, and the levels of regulatory and internal limits corresponding to them are defined in the RAS. Risk appetite framework describes methodology and process for development of RAS, escalation process regarding breaches of predefined in RAS limits and targets, description of responsibilities, timing framework and steering process. In Table 8.1 a risk appetite framework overview example is presented.

For each RAS measure green, amber and red zones of operation should be defined. The green zone is the safe zone, above the internal limit. It can be capped (or floored), if a too high (or a too low) level of the measure is not optimal. For example, if there's too much of liquidity or capital – it is safe from the regulatory requirements' side, but it is sub-optimal from the profitability point of view, which is why RAS should provide borders to avoid usage of resources that is not optimal. On the contrary, the profitability indicators should not be limited as the higher the RoE and the lower the cost to income ratio, the better it is for the bank.

Amber RAS limit is usually equal to the internal steering limit. Capital, liquidity, different types of risk, profitability, etc., should be steered in practice against these levels, meaning that they should be incorporated in all reports and communicated to the regulator. Amber zone is, subsequently, the zone between amber and

https://doi.org/10.1515/9783110669763-011

Table 8.1: Risk appetite framework example.

Risk appetite pillars (goals) and measures/indicators			
Liquidity & Funding	**Capital Adequacy**	**Stable Earnings Growth**	**Stakeholder Confidence**
Be an agile, sustainable bank that has stable and efficient access to funding and liquidity, and can withstand appropriate liquidity related stress, with relevant liquid asset holdings.	Maintain sufficient capital, quantity and quality, substantially over regulatory minimums to cover projected risks in different plausible scenarios.	Be an agile, sustainable bank that maintains its capital adequacy in terms of amount and quality, and hence can withstand appropriate capital related stress.	Be an agile, sustainable bank that is respected and trusted by all its stakeholders and always maintains stakeholder confidence.
– Loan to deposit ratio – Available liquidity minimum – NSFR, LCR – Concentration ratio – Internal funds pricing regime	– CET1, T1, total capital ratios – Leverage ratio	– Earnings volatility – RoE – Return on RWA – Cost to income ratio	– Reputational risk – Outsourcing risk – Compliance risk

red limits. A bank, operating in the amber zone, still does not breach any of the regulatory indicators, although it does not mean that the bank can keep measures in the amber zone for a long time. As a matter of fact, the RAS is shared with the competent authorities; moreover, they should be immediately informed about breaching the internal limit. The bank should elaborate as soon as possible the options for recovery of the breached indicators (recovery plan) and submit them to the supervisors. Also a breach of the amber level (entering in the amber zone) usually triggers an escalation process, followed by appointment of the emergency response team (ERT) by the management board, more frequent and more detailed reporting (to the ERT), testing of availability of other options, and constant dialog between the management board and the regulatory authorities.

With regard to the red levels, a bank should by no means breach them in the going concern case (not a crisis situation). Red level in RAS is usually equal to the amber level of the recovery indicators and triggers the start of a recovery process (see Box 14.1).

For an ALM all levels and zones of relevant indicators are important. They indeed constitute the traffic lights for steering of the balance sheet. ALM may be responsible for calibration (suggestion to the MB) of levels for relevant indicators, such as capital adequacy, leverage ratio levels and some liquidity indicators. ALM may fulfill a function of "4 eyes check," when indicators are calibrated by the risk department (e.g., regarding risk-specific metrics for credit, market, liquidity, operational risk).

Chapter 9
ALM Responsibilities (Full Scope)

On almost all the pillars and measures of the risk appetite framework, ALM may have an impact in different banks. The total list of responsibilities that ALM (or sometimes called Treasury) in different banks is observed to do is described below. However, it does not mean that every bank should try to place all these tasks within ALM/Treasury.

For better representation of the full scope of responsibilities, they can be grouped according to their subject and aim. Aims of tasks can be split into short term and long term. Short-term tasks are operational ones, the usual ALM routine that should be constantly repeated throughout the whole year. Fulfillment of these tasks ensures that on a daily basis banks' operations are within the set limits and banks have enough resources. Long-term tasks are strategic tasks that define the direction the bank is going in, how it is developing. Such tasks usually take more time for execution and therefore are only periodically repeated in order to verify that the bank is developing according to defined strategy. At the same time, they can be split into tasks that aim to ensure the bank's business in conditions as usual (the "going concern" approach), and analysis of its sustainability in cases of stressed conditions (the "gone concern" approach).

The subject of ALM tasks is derived from the definition of asset and liability management and in general corresponds to some pillars in risk appetite framework.

Box 9.1. Definition of Asset and Liability Management

While digging into the question of what exactly the ALM is, it was interesting to consult textbooks starting from the mid-1980s. In the first sources, where the authors touched upon a problem of asset and liability management, the ALM was perceived as a part of banks' strategic planning and was defined as a strategic management instrument for banks' IRR and liquidity risk steering.[1] This definition from today's perspective seems to be too narrow, as an instrument is only one possible mechanism or measure applied in a wider process of management in order to achieve the result. In later books a notion of ALM was perceived in a wider sense, nevertheless, its relation to strategic management still stayed. P. Rose defines asset and liability management as "coordinated and integrated decision-making, considering how an integrated asset and liability portfolio contributes to the firm's broad goals of adequate profitability and acceptable risk."[2] This definition reflects the sense of ALM as a process, which applies actions to reach the bank's goals, although it does not define and limit the scope of tasks that are solved by the ALM.

In contemporary studies and books (after 2002–2006) authors defined asset and liability management more precisely, as very often they were basing it on their own experience of practical work in this area. Among the activities that represent asset and liability management, the professionals

---

1 C. Neil, *An Introduction to Risk Management*, 2nd ed. Prentice-Hall, 1986.

2 P. Rose and S. Hudgins, *Bank Management & Financial Services*, 9th ed. McGraw Hill, 2013.

https://doi.org/10.1515/9783110669763-012

named simultaneously integrated banks' assets, liabilities, and funds management[3] and finding such balance between assets and liabilities that would ensure minimum exposure to price risk,[4] management of IRR and liquidity risk, maximization of the bank's net present value (NPV) and interest income.[5]

Regulatory guidelines almost never provide an explicit definition of asset and liability management, although there are listed components of ALM: determination, implementation, control, and review of asset and liability strategies with aims of achieving financial goals of an organization taking into account the company risk level and other appropriate constraints.[6]

It is recognized that in most of the sources ALM is perceived as a process of coordinated adjustment/changing of assets and liabilities in order to reach their optimal relation, which will ensure fulfillment of banks' aims and tasks. As far as tasks of risk minimization (including IRR) and income (interest income) generation contradict each other, different authors as a criterion for optimal structure of assets and liabilities suggest either maximization of income at a certain level of risk or minimization of risk as a defined income level. Both criteria seem to be correct and applicable at different times (see Part 1) and according to different circumstances in the market, regulatory environment, and specific conditions for a bank. Thus, asset and liability management in general can be defined as *a process of modelling balance sheet and off-balance items and changing their volumes and decomposition in order to achieve banks' goals and targets in different macro-environments and in line with specific banks' resource profile, as well as to fulfill external and internal risk limitations and constraints on liquidity, interest rate, FX risks, and capital adequacy.*

ALM tasks (see Table 9.1) can be split according to its subject into:
- Interest rate, currency, and liquidity risk (further mentioned as ALM risk) management to ensure that a bank acts within external and internal risk limitations and has at all times enough liquidity in all currencies and a sustainable funding plan
- Balance sheet structure steering and targeting by means of deals with necessary maturity, currency, and quality (including the hedging deals) to maintain sufficient capital adequacy in different macro-environments
- Providing of a price benchmarking for lending and borrowing to business lines and, as a result, settlement of the motivation system in order to reach banks' specific goals and ensure stable earnings growth
- Allocation of liquidity, capital, risk levels and interest margin to the bank's business lines and providing transparency about available limits and constraints to the stakeholders

---

3 Ibid.; J.F. Sinkey, *Commercial Bank Financial Management in the Financial-Services Industry*. Prentice Hall, 2002.

4 J.F. Marshall. *Financial Engineering: A Complete Guide to Financial Innovation*. New York Institute of Finance, February 1, 1992.

5 M. Choudhry, *Bank Asset and Liability Management: Strategy, Trading, Analysis*. John Wiley & Sons, 2007.

6 *Standard on Asset-Liability Management*. International Association of Insurance Supervisors, 2006, Standard No. 13.

Table 9.1: ALM tasks.

		ALM risk management	BS structure targeting	Price benchmarking	Resources allocation
Short-term/ tactical tasks		Liquidity buffer management Operational liquidity management Cash and equivalents management Interbank placements Repo operations Securities purchases Derivatives execution FX limiting balances Exchange operations Cash flow analysis Collateral management Counterparty limits control	Capital adequacy steering	FTP curve construction	Liquidity cost calculation
Long-term/ strategic tasks	**Going concern**	Interest rate risk management Interest rate gap modelling Liquidity risk management Contingency planning Balance sheet hedging Determining metrics and limits	Debt issuance Raising long-term funding Securitization Funding and capital planning Defining capital structure	Product pricing Business profitability models Funds transfer pricing Behavioral modelling Maturity matching	NII and NIM forecasting Target RoE setting RoRWA comparison Strategy development RWA and capital allocation Cost of capital definition
	Gone concern	ILAAP execution Liquidity stress testing Cash flow stress testing	ICAAP execution Capital stress testing MREL forecasting Resolution planning Recovery planning		Economic capital calculation and allocation

It is important to note that all the tasks tend to be more interconnected (see Chapter 6 in Part 1).

Descriptions of each ALM task and underlying procedures are precisely provided in regulatory documents and widely explained in textbooks that are devoted to specific topics. However, in order to master one's skills in asset and liability management one should understand the holistic picture and all the interconnections between separate parts. Aiming to give a systemic view and to show a liaison between the ALM tasks and the balance sheet (those assets and liabilities that are meant to be managed), a high-level aggregation is presented in Figure 9.1.

Let's simply assume that a bank's balance sheet contains only cash, a bond, a loan, and an investment in a subsidiary bank (participation) on the asset side and only a deposit, some issued debt and own funds (equity) on the liability and equity side. Each balance sheet item has several characteristics (volume, currency, tenor/maturity, interest rate, etc.). These characteristics define impact of this balance sheet item on the risk profile of the bank. For example, additional volume of loans will require additional funding in order to lend it. At the same time, it will increase amount of credit RWA and decrease capital adequacy ratio (if all the rest is equal). Different characteristics impact different types of risk and are reflected in different metrics and require various instruments from categories defined earlier on ALM tasks. The color coding in Figure 9.1 corresponds to the color coding from Table 9.1 and shows that ALM tasks spread over the whole balance sheet and intercept with each other. These characteristics represent not only inputs for calculation of ALM metrics, but further these ALM metrics will impact characteristics through implementation of management actions. This table should be read from asset or liability sides to the middle of the table, as characteristics of assets and liabilities are used as parts of calculations of metrics, which can then be components for higher level calculations. For example, a loan possesses a characteristic of volume, which will be used in calculations of (a) liquidity metrics (liquidity gap, LCR, NSFR, etc.); (b) capital adequacy metrics (as in multiplication by corresponding risk weight that will constitute risk weighted assets (RWA) amount, which is used in capital adequacy ratio calculation); (c) profitability metrics (as in multiplication with the rate it would give interest income, which is part of the bank's net profit).

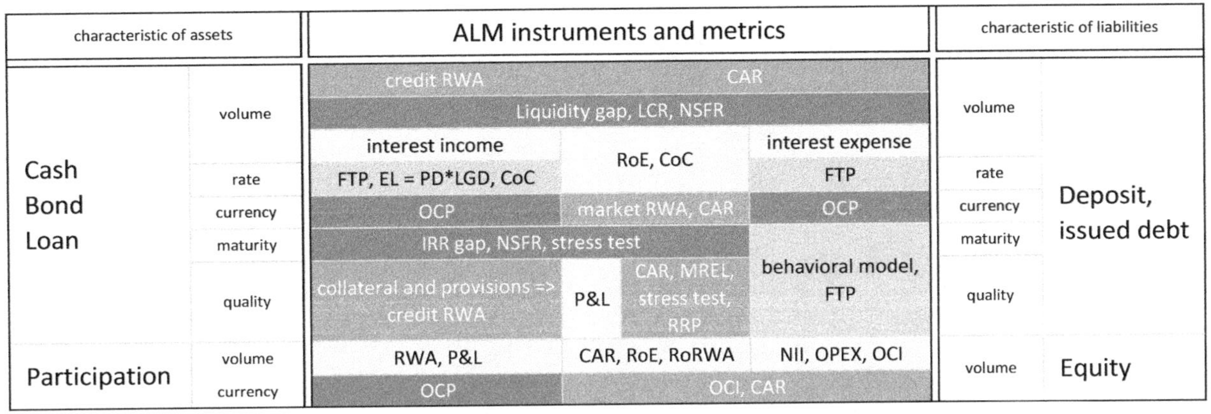

Figure 9.1: ALM metrics impacted by balance sheet items.

Detailed descriptions of the interconnections for different items on the bank's balance sheet are as follows:

A) Loan

This category usually represents the largest part of the asset side of the bank's balance sheet, and includes loans granted to retail and corporate customers, with collaterals and without, with embedded options and plain vanilla ones, overdrafts, interbank loans, including placements in the national bank. Of course, different types of loans require different steering, but their impact on the ALM is driven by same characteristics that are owned by any type of the loans.

A loan is an amount of money provided to a counterparty, so its first and main characteristic is *volume*. This amount is provided in some particular *currency* and is promising to the bank to return interest payments according to a predefined *rate* and to be fully repaid at *maturity* (for simplicity reasons amortization of the loan is included in notion of "maturity"). The *credit quality* of the loan is also important and is defined by many factors, like type of loan, type of borrower, country of the borrower, available collateral, etc.

In order to disburse a loan of a certain volume a bank should check restrictions, set in RAS: does it have enough liquidity, available capital, free legal lending limits? If there are no limitations from the regulatory limits side, a bank should clarify if a loan with its characteristics is beneficial for the bank.

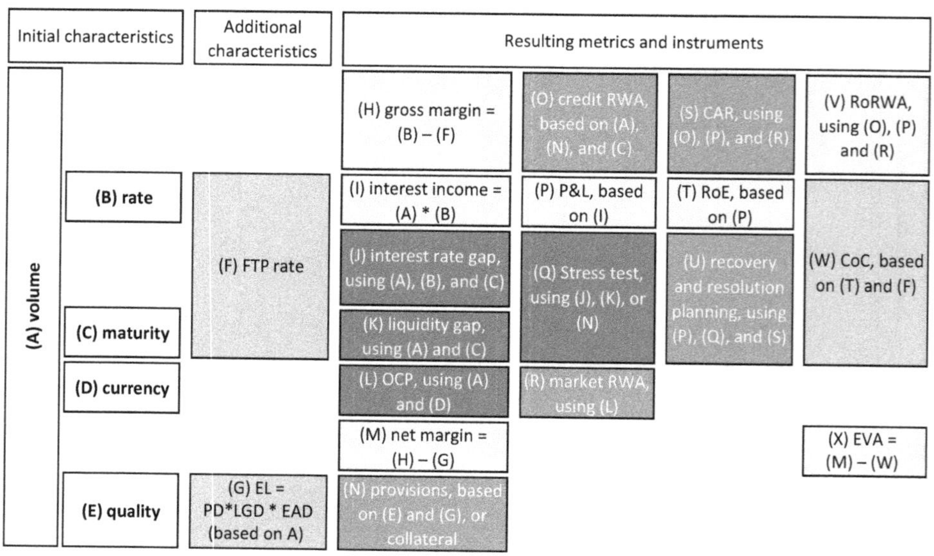

Figure 9.2: ALM metrics impacted by loans.

These checks should be done already in the budgeting process and then the overall loan volume must be checked against the budget, capital, and funding plans. In addition, every loan should be checked against all these metrics if the bank is close to its liquidity or capital limits. In order to confirm that a loan can be disbursed from a liquidity point of view, its volume should be checked against liquidity metrics and instruments, such as cash flow analysis, liquidity gap analysis, LCR, NSFR, loan-to-deposit ratio. To check if there is available capital, impact of the volume and RWA of the loan should be simulated on capital adequacy ratios and large exposure limits. To verify if the loan is beneficial for the bank, special metrics based on its rate should be calculated.

After a loan is disbursed – it is reflected in all the metrics (see Figure 9.2). It should be captured in the core banking system with some additional characteristics: based on its currency and maturity (and type of loan) an *FTP rate* corresponding to this loan is defined, also credit quality is assessed and reflected in assignment of a credit rating and calculation of the *expected loss (EL).*

Having defined (and captured in the system) the main and additional characteristics, it is possible to calculate the metrics needed for ALM:

- For ALM risk management such metrics are:
  - Interest rate gap (a loan impacts it by its volume and type of rate at particular maturity – see Box 2.1 for details)
  - Liquidity gap, liquidity ratios, survival horizon (a loan impacts these metrics by its volume and maturity – see boxes 2.1 and 5.1 for details)
  - Open currency position (OCP) (a loan changes its amount through its volume and currency)

These metrics can be further inputs for stress testing (as liquidity position, interest rate gap, and OCP can be stressed by application of hypothetical macro-economic and individual scenarios – see Box 9.3 for details) and recovery and resolution planning (in part of definition of recovery options or impediments regarding resolution – see Box 14.1 for details).

- For balance sheet structure targeting the capital adequacy is calculated. Capital adequacy ratios are calculated as capital (banks' own funds) divided by risk weighted assets. A loan will have an impact on both sides of this calculation:
  - For every loan the credit RWA are calculated through multiplying its volume by the risk weight, which depends on the type of loan credit quality. For example, according to standardized approach, to placements with the national banks a zero risk weight is commonly applied, for short-term interbank loans at least 20% risk weight is applied,[7] for retail loans in

7 Art. 119 CRR II.

general 75%,[8] and for corporate loans 100%,[9] for overdue loans risk weight can come up to 150%.[10] Possible collaterals (cash collateral, real estate, or rights) will decrease the amount of credit RWA.
  - A loan will also impact RWA through its currency: change in the OCP will impact amount of market RWA.
  - The capital side of the capital adequacy ratio is positively impacted by the interest income from a loan.
  - At the same time capital is negatively affected by loan loss provisions (as they decrease profit/increase loss).
  - If loss provisions were created for a loan, they are deducted from credit RWA.
- Price benchmarking was executed in assigning the FTP rate, that is together with EL and CoC is applied further for new deals (see Box 9.2).
- For resources, allocation income metrics are calculated by:
  - The interest income (multiplication of the volume and the rate of a loan)
  - Interest margins (gross margin is a difference of the rate to the FTP rate, net margin is a difference between the gross margin and EL, economic value added is a difference between the net margin and CoC – see Box 9.2)

It is obvious that interest income is a part of the income statement and will then impact the result of the bank (P&L). P&L constitutes part of own funds and is included in CAR calculations. Based on P&L, RoE is calculated, which is used by shareholders assessing productivity of the bank and comparing it to the market return. RoE is a part of CoC calculations (see Box 9.2). P&L is an important metric, which is also used in stress testing and recovery and resolution planning.

Income (return) of a loan in the absolute amount is not helpful for comparison of several loans, as they might have different risk weights: for these purposes a metric RoRWA is applied. It combines information about profitability and capital consumption. This metric is used on a stage of budgeting when allocating RWA to different business lines/segments/branches.

Box 9.2. Targeting of the Customer Lending Rate

Usually ALM is the department responsible for definition of the principles, how customer rates should be derived. When speaking about loans one should understand that this basic product for customers contains the majority of risks a bank is exposed to: credit risk, liquidity risk, repricing risk, etc., and requires different resources for providing it to customers (funding, capital, resources to cover operational expenses for processing the alignment and disbursement, and then monitoring). Therefore, there are several elements that form the customer rate and several levels of margin that should be considered by the bank in the decision-making.

---

8 Art. 123 CRR II.

9 Art. 122 CRR II.

10 Art. 127 CRR II.

The basic formula for a customer loan rate would be:

$$CR = FTP + EL + CoC + OpEx$$

FTP rate should be assigned for the proper tenor (considering all the installments, amortization of the debt, confirmed period of disbursement, and available options for prolongation and prepayment). Principles of an FTP curve construction are described in Box 4.1.

EL should consider the type of lending product, available collateral, and, basically, the credit rating of the borrower. The latter impacts two parameters, which multiplication defines in theory EL: these are probability of default (PD) and loss given default (LGD). It is more common to define PD according to the rating of each customer, while LGD is very often taken at a particular level (e.g., 60%), which is changed when different market circumstances occur.

CoC is a parameter that charges the borrower also for usage of the most expensive resource of the bank – its own funds. There is no one unique method for defining CoC. One of the possible approaches for its definition is described below. It is obvious that scarcity of own funds is defined by regulatory requirements to capital (the stricter the requirements, the higher the CoC). At the same time, capital itself is not the funding for the loan, so it should be applied only in a small part which represents the consumption of capital adequacy. Taking this into account the usual formula of WACC (weighted average CoC) is transformed: CoC = capital requirement * (WACC – FTP), where capital requirement should be the most binding one among existing capital requirements, WACC represents average cost of different types of capital. Thus, if a bank has equity and subordinated loans, its most binding capital requirement is the one for the total capital, then WACC = equity * RoE * (1 – tax rate) + subordinated loan * its rate. RoE should represent a long-term strategic RoE, which the bank targets, considering the market conditions, its place on the market, and profitability of the peer group. Ideally it should be based on the CAPM model,[11] but for smaller banks this can require using assumptions on the financial institution's β and the premium to the market.

OpEx are defined according to managerial accounting models of the unit costs for loan production. The granularity of determination of these expenses always depends on the technical availability of the bank.

When a bank's credit committee decides on how beneficial a loan for the bank is, it assesses the margins. Gross margin is a difference of the customer rate and the FTP rate. It should always be positive, because in the other case it would mean that the bank attracts funding at a more expensive interest rate, than it grants loans. Net margin is a difference of the gross margin and EL and shows if the customer rate covers not only expenses for funding, but also the credit risk of the loan. Ideally net margin also should be always above zero, but a bank's credit committee can decide on granting the loan, if there are other important factors (like connected business), which can be taken into consideration. Finally, economic value added (EVA) is the difference between the net margin and CoC, and it shows if the loan also covers consumed capital by its interest return.

B) Bond

A bond can be separately pointed out because after a loan it plays the second largest role on the asset side of the balance sheet. This category includes government

11 RoE of the institution = risk-free rate + β * equity risk premium. In practice (and not for ideal markets and banks) as risk-free rate government bond quotes can be used; equity risk premium can be taken from Damodaran's Library for Country Risk Premium (http://pages.stern.nyu.edu/~adamodar/); β if available of the institution should be taken, or can simulated by using pure-play method.

bonds and corporate bonds, bought for liquidity purposes in the banking book and for speculative reasons in the trading book.

A bond, as well as a loan, can be characterized by its *volume* (amount of bonds purchased by the bank) in some particular *currency* that is expected to provide some payments according to a predefined *rate (coupon)* during its life until *maturity (duration). A* bond's credit *quality* is also an unattainable characteristic, which will help to assign two additional characteristics to a bond in order to ensure correct reflection of a bond in ALM methods and instruments (see Figure 9.3).

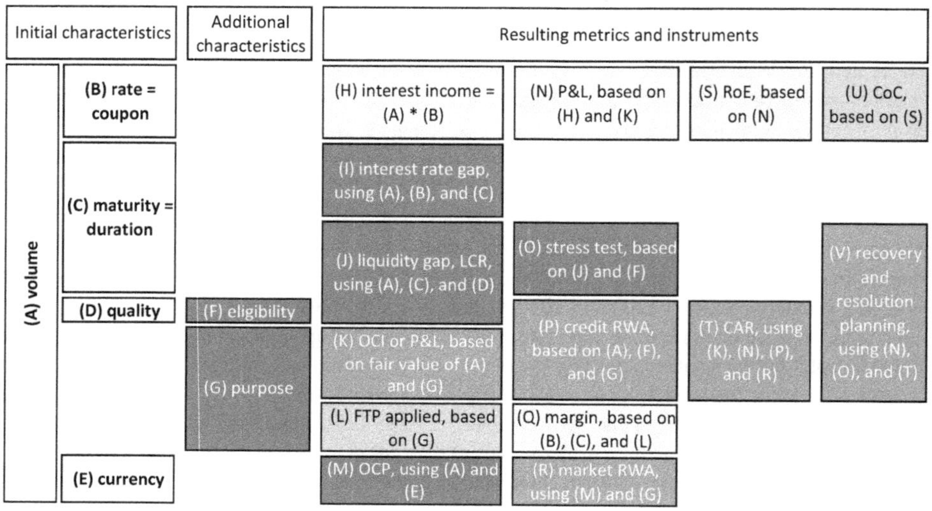

Figure 9.3: ALM metrics impacted by bonds.

These characteristics are the *purpose* of this bond and its *eligibility* for some additional operations. Under purpose mainly the purpose of purchase is understood: it can be purchased as a long-term investment in order to collect contractual cash flows (payments of interest and the principal) – and then it will be accounted at amortized cost and will have the same characteristics as a loan; or it can be purchased with an aim of getting profit (usually accounted in a trading book) – this will lead to constant revaluation of the instrument and accounting its fair value through other comprehensive income (OCI) (if the intention is to sell the bond) or through P&L.[12] Under eligibility of a bond (very much interconnected with quality as a loan characteristic) is meant its ability to act as collateral for the national bank and/or supranational institutions.

Before purchasing a bond all its characteristics should be checked against the budget (is this amount within the planned volume and pricing?) and limits. The limits, as usual, contain liquidity constraints (for how long this bond is purchased, can it be

12 IFRS 9 financial instruments classification.

pledged for liquidity purposes, is it included in liquidity buffer and LCR calculations?), capital limitations (what risk weight will be applied to this bond, is there available capital?) and IRR (how bonds' duration would impact the interest rate gap?).

After purchasing and reflecting the bond in the core banking system ALM methods and metrics will contain the impact of this bond.

- For ALM risk management rather similar to a loan a bond becomes a part of
  - Interest rate gap (a bond impacts it by its volume, type of rate and duration – see Box 2.1 for details).
  - Liquidity gap, liquidity ratios survival horizon (a bond impacts these metrics by its volume, duration, and quality. Depending on the quality of the bond its purchase can impact either negatively, when the bond is not eligible for pledging and liquidity ratios calculations, or neutrally or even positively, if a bond is national bank and LCR eligible).
  - OCP (a bond changes OCP value through its volume and currency).

As mentioned before, these metrics can further be inputs for stress testing (see Box 9.3) and recovery and resolution planning (see Box 14.1).

- For balance sheet structure targeting it is of vital importance that capital adequacy restrictions are fulfilled. As defined earlier, capital adequacy ratios are driven by own funds and RWA – and a bond contributes to both sides of the ratio.
  - To a bond, as to any exposure, a risk weight will be assigned, and it will contribute to credit RWA in amount depending on the issuer type (what is very much interconnected with eligibility and purpose of the bond) and available collateral.
  - A bond will contribute to market RWA by its portion in the OCP, as well as by its revaluation depending on the purpose of purchase).
  - The capital side of the capital adequacy ratio is impacted by risk provisions (if they are required to be created for the bond) and, more often, by change in P&L (will be impacted by interest/coupons received) and OCI (which is part of regulatory own funds and among other encompass revaluations of purchased securities).
- Price benchmarking is slightly touched by a bond: only general procedures are applied, like an FTP rate applied to the bond (as it should be applied to every balance sheet item), or a bond's contribution to P&L will impact RoE and CoC for the next periods.
- Profitability metrics for proper resources allocation will be in general impacted by a bond: interest income itself (sum of the coupons received, also which could be represented by multiplication of the volume and the rate of a bond) and the interest margin (gross margin as a difference between the rate and the FTP rate). Then the chain will be the same as described earlier: interest income is a part of the bank's result (P&L), which is a component of RoE and, subsequently, CoC.

Box 9.3. Stress Testing

Bank for International Settlements[13] defines stress tests as simulation exercises conducted to assess the resilience of a bank to a hypothetical scenario. The IMF[14] describes it as a quantitative "what if" exercise to estimate the resilience of banks if certain shocks were to materialize. Based on definitions it is clear that a stress test does not provide a forecast of a bank's performance under stress, rather, it aims to evaluate the impact on the bank of a specific stress scenario based on given assumptions. In terms of degree of severity, a scenario can be described as either "baseline" or "adverse":

(a) Baseline scenario: a set of economic and financial conditions that are generally consistent with the projection of a likely path for a bank's development (a budget can also play a role of the baseline scenario). The baseline scenario usually does not lead to a stressed result.

(b) Adverse scenario: a set of economic and financial conditions that are designed to stress the performance of a bank in the base scenario. The level of stress is significantly stronger than in a baseline scenario. Stress factors could be drawn from historical events or hypothetically created.

First stress tests were conducted in the early 1990s by individual banks for internal risk management purposes. These exercises were small-scale, only to evaluate trading portfolios. Later Basel II also required that banks subject their credit portfolios in the banking book to stress tests.

These stress tests were all *solvency stress tests*, aiming to assess banks' capital adequacy as the core banks' ability to absorb losses and continue its business.

During the period of development of stress testing, stress tests expanded from the ones that focus on *individual banks* and that can be carried out by banks themselves (also named *a bottom-up approach*, where all stress test parameters are defined by a bank) to *system wide stress tests* conducted by central banks and/or supervisory agencies (*top-down approach*, when the assumptions, models, etc., are defined by supervisory/regulatory authorities). The latter ones were introduced by the IMF and the World Bank prior to the global financial crisis, formalized by BIS[15] and first were performed in the United States and the EU in 2009. System-wide stress tests started to be conducted on a regular basis since 2011. Although solvency stress tests were still dominant across banking systems, the necessity of stress tests to consider funding and liquidity risk was also outlined. Liquidity risk started to be either modelled in the form of shocks to funding costs in solvency stress tests or covered separately in targeted *liquidity stress test* exercises. Different types of stress tests will have different time horizons: a solvency stress test covers from two to five years, liquidity stress tests are much shorter (e.g., one day to a few months).

The 2011 and 2014 stress test exercises featured a hurdle capital rate, which determined whether a bank passed or failed the exercise and was used for identifying possible capital shortfalls and recapitalization needs. In 2016[16] the hurdle rate was eliminated, but supervisors started using the results of the stress test to assess banks' forward-looking capital planning and to determine possible capital needs as a result of SREP.[17] During that time, a systemwide stress test was using only *a static balance sheet* assumption (balance sheet is assumed to remain constant over the stress test horizon in terms of total volume, maturity, and product mix), while for internal reasons (e.g., incorporation of

13 P. Baudino, R. Goetschmann, J. Henry, K. Taniguchi, and W. Zhu, Stress-Testing Banks – A Comparative Analysis, FSI Insights on Policy Implementation No. 12, Financial Stability Institute BIS, November 2018.

14 Macrofinancial Stress-Testing – Principles and Practices, International Monetary Fund, August 2012.

15 Principles for Sound Stress Testing Practices and Supervision, BCBS, May 2009.

16 2016 EU-Wide Stress Test Methodological Note, EBA, 24 February 2016.

17 Guidelines on common procedures and methodologies for the supervisory review and evaluation process (SREP), EBA, 19 December 2014, EBA/GL/2014/13.

a stress test in capital planning and budgeting) a *dynamic balance sheet* assumption (the size, composition, or risk profile of a bank's balance sheet can vary over the stress test horizon) can be used.

Evolution of the stress test was summarized in updated principles for sound stress testing in 2018, but there are still open questions and controversial topics that will be addressed in new updates. The challenges are related to:

- Considering the increasing awareness of global interconnectedness, spillover, and contagion effects that have not yet reached a mature stage
- Enhancing the interaction between solvency and liquidity stress tests, with liquidity stress testing developing further into financial system-wide stress testing
- Developing new models to address emerging risks, such as cyber-security and climate change
- Increasing transparency on how to derive capital buffers from stress test results
- Moving from static balance sheet approach to dynamic balance sheet approach

C) Equity Participations

Equity participations or investments in other entities are equity on the asset side of the balance sheet. They can be significant (and be treated like own funds of the bank) or insignificant in relation to a bank's balance sheet or equity (and then they will have more in common with loans or bonds).

Any investment is characterized by *volume* and *currency*. Of course, for decision to invest (and to hold or to sell) the profitability of investment should be assessed. As for profitability assessment, different approaches can be applied (if only this is not an exchange-traded stock), the *yield* becomes already an additional characteristic for a participation. Also, profitability of investment is usually assessed on a horizon of time – so *time* should be already added to a list of characteristics (see Figure 9.4).

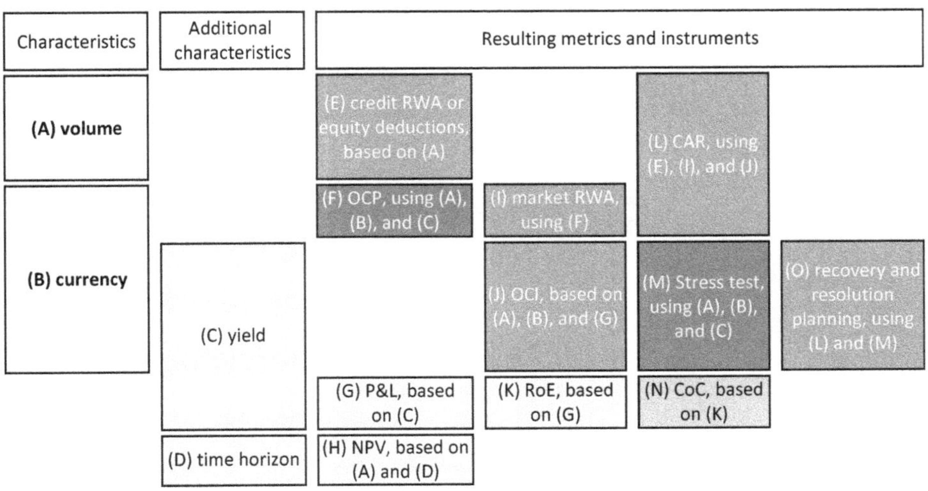

Figure 9.4: ALM metrics impacted by equity participations.

Participations impact mainly profitability and capital adequacy metrics, although in other ALM areas they should also be carefully considered.

- For ALM risk management
  - In part of liquidity it is only important to check that investments are not over-consuming available liquidity.
  - In part of interest rate gap, as far as participations are not interest-bearing assets, they will not impact the IRR position.
  - With regard to OCP, it is important to know that any investment is reflected in the consolidated IFRS balance sheet in the currency of the balance sheet (converted with an exchange rate at the moment of purchase), and any revaluations of participations due to currency changes will be reflected in the OCI.
  - If the investment is a company with its own assets and liabilities and with currency different to the parent bank's currency – then when calculating a consolidated balance sheet – these subsidiary's assets and liabilities will contribute to the group's OCP through structural currency position stemming from the eliminated capital on the consolidation level. There's a regulatory guidance, which explains how parent companies may apply for waivers, or hedge this structural poition.[18]

Participations are also subject to stress testing, mainly in part of their future profitability, as well as part of recovery and resolution planning, especially when participation is a bank, to which resolution rules are applied.

- Regarding balance sheet structure targeting, participations contribute a lot to capital adequacy calculations.
  - If it is a small investment (less than 10% of the bank's own funds[19]) – then it will be included in credit RWA. Its risk weight will be 250%, if no specific case is applicable.[20]
  - If it exceeds 10% of the bank's own funds (and consolidated) – the amount exceeding the threshold will be risk weighted, but at the same time the equity of the participation will be deducted from the group equity (it will not increase the group equity in consolidation).
  - The capital side in capital adequacy calculation will also be impacted by the OCI and goodwill (for goodwill accounting see Chapter 16.6).

18 Guidelines on the treatment of structural FX under Article 352(2) of Regulation (EU) No 575/2013 (CRR), EBA/GL/2020/09, EBA, 1 July 2020.

19 Art. 48 CRR II.

20 Art. 133 CRR II, Art. 89(3) CRR II.

- OCI contains effects of two different revaluations of participations:
  - As participations are reflected at the parent balance sheet at a historical rate, but the exchange rate fluctuated all the time for participations in foreign currencies, this revaluation will be reflected in OCI.
  - Assets and liabilities are consolidated at "closing" FX rate (actual FX rate at the end of the period), but accumulated retained earnings of subsidiary were accounted at average FX rate – these differences, between average and "closing" rates, will also become a part of the OCI.
- Goodwill is the difference between the book value and the price, at which the subsidiary has been purchased and will be deducted from the group's capital. Goodwill decreases over the years, after performance of annual subsidiaries' impairment tests.

- Price benchmarking area of ALM should solve a question – what FTP rate to apply to this type of assets with undefined maturity, and what would be its appropriate interest margin? The chain of metrics until definition of CoC is applicable also to participations: their inputs for P&L and, thus, RoE will impact CoC for the next periods.
- ALM uses participations' characteristics a lot while solving its tasks in the area of resource allocation: they are not only banks' general calculations (which are certainly impacted by revaluations of investments or retained earnings of subsidiaries) of the bank's result (P&L), RoE and CoC. ALM sometimes solves questions of necessity of investment or feasibility of purchasing/selling/merging a subsidiary. NPV is one of the possible calculated metrics, in a row with liquidity and capital considerations.

D) Cash

Although cash and cash equivalents don't earn any income to a bank, they can hardly be avoided among banking operations. Cash does not contain many characteristics (only *volume* and *currency*), however it acts as a balancing line in all calculations, so it will definitely impact all the ALM areas described earlier (see Figure 9.5).

Amount of cash and equivalents will directly impact some of the metrics (especially in ALM risk management and balance sheet targeting): liquidity gap, liquidity ratios, OCP, capital adequacy ratios, and stress testing. The higher the amount of cash, the higher the level of available liquidity. In capital adequacy calculations, cash is risk-neutral, so it will not change the capital adequacy ratio. As for stress testing, cash will represent the level of available liquidity, which will be consumed by cash at the very first moment of stress.

At the same time, some of the metrics (as in the case of price benchmarking and resources allocation) will be impacted by cash indirectly. For price benchmarking cash will not only be in a row with participations and other undefined maturity

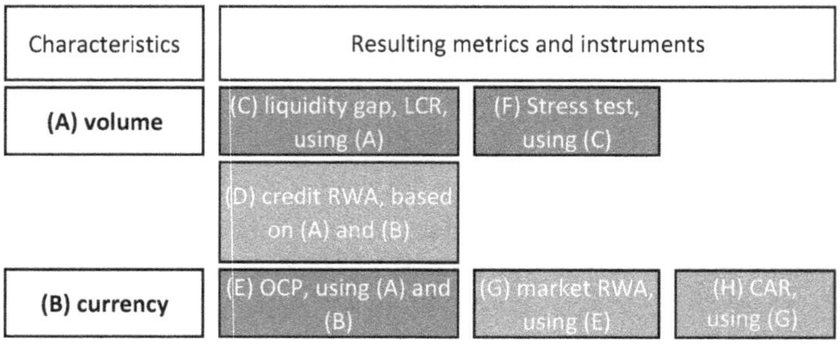

Figure 9.5: ALM metrics impacted by cash.

products for definition and assignment of a proper FTP rate. It will also impact FTP rates of some liabilities, like deposits, for which there are obligatory requirements to keep mandatory reserves (usually at a current account with the Central bank – and here for simplicity reasons are considered in cash description), and thus a lower amount can be invested in loans, bonds, or other participations.

E) Deposit

A deposit represents a major part of liabilities. It can be a customer deposit or an interbank deposit, with particular time to maturity or with undefined maturity (like savings and current accounts). All these deposits have the same types of characteristics for ALM needs. Moreover, issued debt by the bank – although having quite different procedures before getting the funds – possesses the same characteristics and, therefore, can be described in the same section with a deposit.

As a reflection of a loan, a deposit can be characterized by its *volume* in some particular *currency* for which the bank is expected to pay interest according to a predefined *rate* and to fully repay the debt at *maturity*. The *purpose* of the deposit also plays an important role and depending on its purpose, will be a driver for different metrics. The *type* of a deposit (retail, corporate, interbank, MREL eligible, subordinated, etc.) is sometimes a consequence of the purpose, with which the deposit was raised, and is important for evaluation of an impact on metrics.

A decision on raising a deposit (or any funds in general) comes from the budget, where all asset and liability positions were checked on compliance with regulatory requirements, or from liquidity position (especially when there are sudden deviations from the budget).

Also, an instrument that influences the decision for raising funds is an FTP rate, based on a bank's liquidity needs for different maturities. This would be one more additional characteristic for a deposit to consider its impact on ALM metrics (see Figure 9.6).

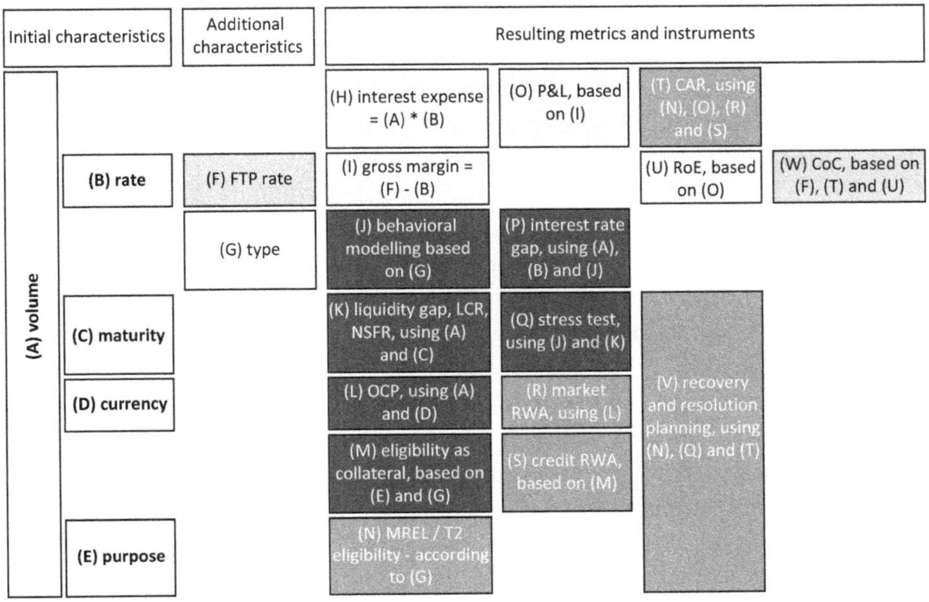

Figure 9.6: ALM metrics impacted by deposits.

- For ALM risk management a deposit will be a part of
  - Interest rate gap (a deposit impacts it by its volume and type of rate at particular maturity – see Box 2.1 for details)
  - Liquidity gap, liquidity ratios, survival horizon (a deposit impacts these metrics by its volume and maturity – see Boxes 2.1 and 5.1 for details)
  - OCP (a deposit changes its amount through its volume and currency)

As for deposit's maturity, depending on its type either its actual maturity will be taken, or a calculated one via application of behavioral models for undefined maturity products. Its volume also can be adjusted due to obligations to keep some "cash" reserve and not to use the whole amount for lending.

As a part of collateral management it will be possible to define deposit's eligibility as collateral for some asset side products. It will in turn be used for adjusting stress test scenarios. Other inputs for stress testing and recovery and resolution planning are, as previously mentioned, the interest, liquidity, and FX risk metrics.

- Within balance sheet structure targeting the deposit's purpose and type are defined as:
  - Plain vanilla funding for liquidity needs only
  - Or it is already a MREL eligible long-term interbank funding to comply with MREL targets
  - Or it is a subordinated loan to be accounted for as part of T2 capital

  - Or it is even a quasi-equity instrument – a perpetual loan – raised for improvement of T1 capital
  - If a deposit plays a role of collateral for some loan – it will be able to decrease RWA and loan loss provisions – meaning lower negative impact on the P&L, or as part of OCP will impact market RWA
  - If eligibility criteria for inclusion in MREL or own funds are met – then the deposit will positively impact the MREL ratio or the capital adequacy ratio nominator
- Price benchmarking with regard to a deposit is executed at the moment of assigning the FTP rate. In order to assign the correct FTP rate a deposit's maturity should be defined (using statistical models if needed). Also it is necessary to check its possible relation to some loan/type of asset business[21] – if there is a case of exemptions from the common FTP rule, and for related deals (with equal volumes on asset and liability sides) an average internal rate between the asset side and the liability side of the deal is applied.

It is important to note that if this type of deposit provides a theoretically unlimited amount of funding, it can be used for defining the future FTP rates.

- The newly defined FTP curve, of course, will be an instrument for resource allocation, as it will allow to calculate not only the interest expense on the deposit (multiplication of the volume and the rate of a deposit), but also the gross margin (difference of the FTP rate and the deposit's rate). This will further impact other income metrics, such as the bank's result (P&L), RoE, and CoC.

F) Equity

There is no need to define characteristics for equity to show a linkage to ALM methods and metrics. In fact, equity is already a result of characteristics of other balance sheet items. As it could be captured from the descriptions mentioned earlier– equity contains retained earnings, which means that profit or loss is accumulated every year and is included in equity. It is impacted not only by interest income or expense, widely mentioned before, but also by commissions and fees, operating expenses, and taxes.

Equity is a base for capital adequacy calculations, although equity in accounting and own funds used for calculation of capital adequacy ratios differ, according to rules defined in CRR. Own funds are included in MREL eligible instruments.

Equity is the main component for RoE calculations and setting profitability targets for subsidiaries and the bank itself.

21 It can be a deposit for a purpose of some loan, or it can be a deposit line (from a supranational organization or even national government) provided to the bank to stimulate some particular lending business.

Chapter 10
ALM Operating Model

Of course, no Treasury/ALM desk could have full responsibility for all the tasks listed in the previous chapter, as some of the functions are contradicting each other and raising conflicts of interest. For example, one department can't set limits on positions and execute deals for these positions, construct an internal yield curve, and make deals with margin to this curve. In order to exclude obvious contradictory tasks in practice different combinations are observed, among which there are the two quite contrasted options: Treasury as a front office and ALM desk as a middle office.

Front office is a part of a company where revenues are generated, and it consists of employees who come into contact with clients. Front office Treasury also specializes in external markets and interaction with counterparties. When the ALM department is arranged as a front office, the strategic and controlling functions are excluded. It is actually necessary to avoid a conflict of interest, when the same unit defines the rules for deal execution, sets limits and controlling metrics, determines prices, elaborates methodology of positions assessment, and at the same time executes deals with an aim of profit generation.

In addition to eliminating conflict of interest (what is, obviously, a first priority – and is strictly monitored by supervising authorities), establishment of the division in this view has another explanation: a front office function and a controlling/strategic function require quite different managerial experience and approach from the responsible manager: style for leading an analytical team will be more grounded and even cautious, when a team aimed for active operations should be led in a more active way.

Moreover, a front office ALM desk is more frequently a profit center. As having key performance indicators (KPIs) on profit from trading operations (even for a Banking book) will give more incentives for liquidity managers (of course not everyone even in a Front office ALM desk will be actively trading on financial markets). In Table 10.1 the functions of the front office ALM desk are non-shaded.

On the contrary, a middle office is a part of a company that manages risk and calculates profits and losses. Middle office Treasury is responsible mainly for strategic balance sheet management. It is again possible to avoid a clear conflict of interest in this case, and ALM desk fulfills an analytical function, providing to the bank's management board all the necessary information for correct decision-making. In Table 10.2 the tasks of the middle office ALM desk are non-shaded.

Nevertheless, the definition of the type of operating model for the ALM desk and construction of its function according to it is only the first step on the way to avoiding conflicts of interest. In practice, some of the tasks may be transferred to one or another department, which has close functions, as it may be wrong to assume that if on the

https://doi.org/10.1515/9783110669763-013

Table 10.1: Front office Treasury operating model.

		ALM risk management	BS structure targeting	Price benchmarking	Resources allocation
Short-term/ tactical tasks		Liquidity buffer management Operational liquidity management Cash and equivalents management Interbank placements Repo operations Securities purchases Derivatives execution FX balances limiting Exchange operations Cash flows analysis Collateral management Counterparty limits control	Capital adequacy steering	FTP curve construction	Liquidity cost calculation
Long-term/ strategic tasks	**Going concern**	Interest rate risk management Interest rate gap modelling Liquidity risk management Contingency planning Balance sheet hedging Determining metrics and limits	Debt issuance Raising long-term funding Securitization Funding and capital planning Defining capital structure	Product pricing Business profitability models Funds transfer pricing Behavioral modelling Maturity matching	NII and NIM forecasting Target RoE setting RoRWA comparison Strategy development RWA and capital allocation Cost of capital definition
	Gone concern	ILAAP execution Liquidity stress-testing Cash flow stress-testing	ICAAP execution Capital stress-testing MREL forecasting Resolution planning Recovery planning		Economic capital calculation and allocation

Table 10.2: Middle office Treasury operating model.

		ALM risk management	BS structure targeting	Price benchmarking	Resources allocation
Short-term/ tactical tasks		Liquidity buffer management Operational liquidity management Cash and equivalents management Interbank placements Repo operations Securities purchases Derivatives execution FX balances limiting Exchange operations Cash flows analysis Collateral management Counterparty limits control	Capital adequacy steering	FTP curve construction	Liquidity cost calculation
Long-term/ strategic tasks	**Going concern**	Interest rate risk management Interest rate gap modelling Liquidity risk management Contingency planning Determining metrics and limits Balance sheet hedging	Debt issuance Raising long-term funding Securitization Funding and capital planning Defining capital structure	Product pricing Business profitability models Funds transfer pricing Behavioral modelling Maturity matching	NII and NIM forecasting Target RoE setting RoRWA comparison Strategy development RWA and capital allocation Cost of capital definition
	Gone concern	ILAAP execution Liquidity stress-testing Cash flow stress-testing	ICAAP execution Capital stress-testing MREL forecasting Resolution planning Recovery planning		Economic capital calculation and allocation

first sight there are no conflicting tasks in the responsibilities list of the department, the conflict of interest is fully avoided. It is necessary to investigate the full reporting line, as the board member to which this department reports can be responsible for other departments with which functions there will be conflict of interest, or to have private aims, partially contradicting ALM.

Chapter 11
ALM Inside a Risk Management Triangle

Governance and oversight framework for balance sheet risk must revolve around an operating model that provides efficient and effective interaction and liaison between Finance, Treasury (here as a Trading Desk), and Risk functions. So, reporting lines and organization structure for these departments – the three areas of the bank most closely concerned with the balance sheet risk – must be the "right" ones. The balance sheet risk "triumvirate" view of the three suggests they are peers, and therefore must be organized as such. But until they compete for the ALM function – the result is far from efficient.

According to competent authorities' guidelines, "the governing body . . . to avoid potential conflicts of interest should ensure that there is adequate separation of responsibilities in key elements of the risk management process. Banks should have [risk] identification, measurement, monitoring and control functions . . . sufficiently independent from risk-taking functions of the bank."[1] "Without prejudice to the responsibilities assigned under the applicable national company law, the management body in its supervisory function should . . . oversee the implementation and maintenance of a code of conduct or similar and effective policies to identify, manage and mitigate actual and potential conflicts of interest."[2]

Practical experience of many banks often shows that the governing head for the ALM unit rather depends on the personality heading either department than on the functional reasons. Nevertheless, there are some undeniable arguments for and against including ALM in one or another department of the bank's organizational framework, in particular in the Risk Department, Trading Desk, and Financial Department. Already disclosing the conclusion, the arguments against inclusion are too sufficient, so uniting of ALM with either of the traditional banking units is impossible. Detailed analysis and argumentation are described below.

Each of the tasks or functions taken alone can be a bit modified and assigned to the responsibility of one of the major traditional business units: either of Risks, or of the Treasury-Trading Desk, or of Finance. In order to check existence of conflicts of interests Table 11.1 compares high-level tasks of the mentioned departments.

Functions in the table are intentionally named pointing out the same phenomena, although different in some words. In the past there often have been doubts that it was possible to assign all the functions and tasks of ALM to any of the units mentioned above. Seemingly close sounding could make a board member from the business in some small and developing banks confused by ALCO reports from ALM, Trading Desk

1 BCBS standard on interest rate risk in the banking book, BIS, April 2016.
2 Guidelines on internal governance EBA/GL/2017/11, EBA, 21 March 2018.

https://doi.org/10.1515/9783110669763-014

Table 11.1: Comparison of ALM tasks with Risk, Finance, and Trading Desk tasks.

ALM	Risk	Trading	Finance
ALM risk management	Risk assessment	Execution of deals	Profitability analysis
BS structure targeting	Limiting positions/ portfolios	Funding strategy development	Budgeting
Price benchmarking	Models validation, stress testing	Quoting of rates	Deviations analysis
Resources allocation	Economic capital evaluation	Earning income	Profit calculation

and Risk representatives: “Do I understand you correctly, that you are speaking about the same things?” – he might have asked. Yes, definitely, the notions and definitions are used the same, but in some specific words a huge difference is concealed. The similarities and differences of these departments, as well as possible virtues and drawbacks of ALM inclusion in each of them are disclosed further.

It can be seen in Table 11.1 that in terms of ALM risk management all four considered units are participants of the process. At the same time, the Risk Department is the first processor of information, analyzes these risks, and their level for separate positions/portfolios. ALM is a consumer of the results of Risk and offers suggestions/tools for managing identified risks (if they were identified). The Trading Desk then carries out risk management transactions proposed by the ALM and approved by the appropriate collegial body. Finally, Finance considers the risk management deals in overall result of the bank and separately by banking units.

The function of balance sheet structure targeting is also performed by all selected units with a different level of involvement in the process. The Trading Desk, having information about the possibilities of raising funds in the financial market, provides the necessary information to construct a funding plan. Finance receives input data from business units and forms a budget and/or a business plan. Risk imposes restrictions on positions and portfolios in terms of risk metrics (captured also in RAS). ALM makes suggestions on adjusting the balance sheet structure in order to obtain a higher interest margin while fulfilling regulatory restrictions on capital adequacy and liquidity level.

The price benchmarking topic (internal pricing and defining prices for customers) also combines inputs from all the departments. The Trading Desk has information about the level of rates in the market and can provide input data for calculations, in particular, for constructing an internal FTP curve. ALM determines the principles of transfer pricing, builds the internal FTP curve, and defines rules for determining the minimum client rate (and the margin of the transaction). The forecast of FTP rates and, accordingly, client rates Finance uses for budgeting and long-term business planning. Risk is indirectly involved in this task: by checking ALM models (see Box 11.1), or by evaluating the cost of risk for products bearing credit risk (which is a component of the price for the client).

Box 11.1. Lines of Defense

Based on its tasks and responsibilities there's a standard place for ALM/Treasury within the three lines of defense against risk in a bank (based on bank's best practice), see Table 11.2.

Table 11.2: Lines of defense.

Business lines	Make deals (generate risk) Are not lines of defense
1st line of defense ALM/Treasury	Manages balance sheet (FTP, target structure, hedging) Forecasts positions Constructs models
2nd line of defense Risk	Measures and analyzes ALM risk Controls limits and validates models Prepares reports
3rd line of defense Internal audit	Internally audits the 1st and the 2nd lines of defense

One of the key trends of recent years in banking practice has become the organization of the bank's divisions in the format of three lines of defense. A unit which makes a transaction is always preceding any line of defense. Most often this is a business unit that creates positions under credit / market risk.

ALM/Treasury also can be a department that makes the deals (front-office ALM desk), but still it will be considered as the first line of defense, as its aim is to defend the balance sheet from risk. ALM is responsible for suggestion of risk management solutions, as well as for creation of models for execution of its other functions, including price targeting, FTP curve construction and margin allocation principles, managing interest rate and FX risk. Any unit making a transaction is guided by approved ALM models and tools. By defining the responsibility of business units, ALM itself becomes a "defender" of the bank.

There is a normal practice in the bank, to have "4-eyes check" (when the "second pair of eyes" comes from another department, namely from the Risk Department). This "4-eyes check" includes validation of models, confirmation of their appropriateness, and back-testing, that is done by means of imposing and controlling limits, measuring and analyzing risks. The second line of defense verifies the correctness of the application of risk restrictions by business lines and the first line of defense and prepares reports on transactions.

The third line of defense is represented by an internal audit that is a unit which assesses the correctness and good faith of the implementation of its functions by other units. In other words, the internal audit verifies that the first and second lines of defense act in accordance with documents officially approved by the collegial bodies, and the documents describe all the features of the processes and reflect the best international practices.

It is also often admitted that there is the 4th line of defense: supervisory authorities are also fulfilling an audit function and comparison of banks' risk governance to the defined standards. This function is executed during SREP and specific on-site inspections, and is protecting not only an individual bank, but also the national economy overall.

The task of resources allocation is, of course, based on financial result (including segment results) and is calculated by Finance. ALM determines methodology for distribution of FTP margins between business segments, for ALM result ("internal bank") calculation, for allocation of RWA between business lines and subsidiaries, etc. In relation to the latter, allocation methods vary in different banks, but one of the criteria for allocation may be the need for economic capital. The calculation of the required economic capital for the bank as a whole and for business segments, in particular, is carried out by Risk. Thus, Risk is also indirectly involved in the task of resources allocation.

Although there are interconnections – it is not a reason to combine functions of any of the two departments in one unit. Below ALM is opposed to other departments, whereas possible and frequently observed conflicts of interest are outlined.

Precise investigation of the *ALM and Risk* functions shows that uniting both would lead to at least two conflicts of interest.

First, the assessing unit wouldn't be able to evaluate risks impartially. After the unit implements risk management measures, in other words, does the deals, it is natural that the management of the bank would expect the decrease of risks as a result. As far as this exact unit provides the assessment of risks – it would be prone to show the improvement, regardless of the real risk dynamics. ALM even does not have to actively trade/do the deals. As said above, combining of the function of assessment and decision-making can potentially lead to a conflict of interest.

Second, it's highly probable that the united department (Risk and ALM) would be aware of the obstacles/difficulties/peculiarities, connected with some risk management instruments and, thus, could intentionally diminish the risks in its assessment in order to avoid usage of inconvenient instruments. In other words, no risks – no need for measures. Therefore, this unit would tend to get such a result of risks evaluation, so that it would have to apply only the most convenient risk management instruments.

Besides, in addition to risk management ALM fulfills the function of internal yield curve (FTP rates) construction. This function obviously has nothing to do with Risk and can't be assigned to it. At the same time, it's not possible to separate this function from the ALM as FTP is in fact one of the means of risk and asset and liability management.

Therefore, the arguments against including ALM into Risk are significant, and the latter unit can't include the former one in the bank's organizational framework.

When assessing possibilities to unite *Trading Desk and ALM* it can be concluded that both departments execute similar functions by changing the balance sheet structure and eliminating the balance sheet risk (by means of bonds or derivatives, for example). As far as this unit lends and borrows in the financial market it can immediately fulfill all decisions for ALM. Moreover, dealing with financial markets helps to better understand the market situation and leads to more up-to-the-moment FTP curve construction. These reasons simplify execution of the ALM and make the bank more flexible and adaptive to the changing environment. Although also in this situation many conflicts of interest appear.

First, as the Trading Desk is in charge for operations in financial markets, including trading operations, and is a profit-center (that is usually the case), it can use limits and instruments, approved for liquidity management, for achieving its own result. For example, if some bond issue (or if any other instrument as well) is small or this counterparty is internally limited, but extremely attractive for investment, this bond is more likely to be acquired in the trading portfolio, and not in the liquidity management portfolio. If ALM is not a profit center, a conflict of interest will result in the fact that all free resources of the unit will be allocated to active trading, and mandatory liquidity will be placed in the lowest-performing (and currently in many countries unprofitable) asset – in interbank deposits/nostro accounts in central banks (currently with negative interest rates). Such actions and decisions will lead, at a minimum, to inefficient liquidity buffer management, and in some cases even expose the bank to liquidity risk.

Second, there is the same conflict of interest that was already mentioned in the case of combining ALM and Risk. As far as the Trading Desk knows the cost and peculiarities of instruments in the market, by acting as a unit that is in charge for recommending risk management measures it can point out only those ones that are beneficial and convenient for it. A limited (but attractive) bond issue can also be an example here.

The third conflict of interest is related to FTP. Even if the FTP curve is constructed based on the market approach (based on market quotes available in any information systems) and the information for constructing the curve is provided in any case by the Trading Desk, funding principles (i.e., assigning a rate on the curve of a certain tenor for certain types of transactions) can not be determined by the unit making this transaction. A shift of a tenor in favor of a better rate will mean the unit making this transaction will deliberately redistribute income from other units. If the FTP curve is constructed based on the marginal approach, as recommended by the EBA[3] (based on the estimated rates for raising each additional unit of funds), the Trading Desk will affect not only the method of applying FTP rates, but also the rates themselves (as this method concludes subjectivity of assessment). Thus, in this case, the conflict of interest only increases.

Overall, the Trading Desk provides operational management, while ALM (especially with the middle-office operating model) provides strategic decisions about funding, liquidity, capital, interest rates, risk-return trade-off and is responsible for less volatile strategic positions. The crucial point is that short- and long-term strategies contradict each other: they have different aims, different risks and need different pools of resources. In addition, if the ALM unit is a profit center (in other words

3 Guidelines on Liquidity Cost Benefit Allocation, EBA, October 2010.

its aim is to gain maximum of profit) then a larger conflict of interest arises between the Trading Desk and the ALM. The Trading Desk tends to make positions under risk, as far as ALM aims to manage risk. The bigger the ALM and Trading Desk portfolios, the sharper the problem of different interests of the units.

Consequently, including ALM into the Trading Desk ("external" Treasury) will be incorrect due to major conflicts of interest, and making ALM not a profit-center does not help to overcome them.

When analyzing the responsibilities of *Finance*, one can conclude that this unit has functions that are fully compatible with the tasks of *ALM*. ALM includes forecasting of balance sheet structure, obligatory liquidity and capital adequacy ratios, funding needs – therefore, high quality and in-time execution of asset and liability management function enhances the process of financial planning and budgeting. Transfer pricing also in part of forecasting the future interest rates (and margins) can be considered as a part of strategic management and product pricing. Moreover, Finance always possesses the holistic picture of the bank's balance sheet and the most complete managerial accounting data that simplifies the analysis and helps to discover misbalanced assets and liabilities structures.

Nevertheless, in some cases, close cooperation with Finance may adjust the role of ALM as an independent division.

Conflict of interest arises due to multi-directional goals within the same unit. Traditionally, one of the Finance Department's KPIs is budget target for banks' result. If the financial result of the bank is worse than planned in the budget, Finance would find ways to improve it and would tend to skew the priorities of tasks of ALM. In particular, one can expect that with an increase in risk appetite (on the contrary to the thesis "no risk – no money!") – by means of additional interest rate (or market/currency) risk exposures and with a hope for a favorable change of market conditions, the bank will be able to additionally earn on the "gap" of maturity/currency positions. ALM, whose mission is to prevent the bank from taking significant risk (also in part of IRRBB management, see Box 11.2), in this particular case will be interested in good performance of its unit. That would mean that ALM will not prevent additional risk taking.

As a conclusion, ALM can hardly be considered a part of the Finance due to the conflict of aims inside the unit.

Box 11.2. IRRBB Management

An interest rate is a characteristic of almost all balance sheet items (as described in Chapter 9), and a bank's result and long-term value are dependent on the interest rates.

IRRBB refers to the current or prospective risk to the bank's capital and earnings arising from adverse movements in interest rates that affect the bank's banking book positions.[4] The

4 SPR 31 IRRBB, effective as of 15 December 2019, the Basel Framework, BIS, 2020.

threat of negative implications because of adverse interest rate changes can come from two directions:

- First, the interest rate sensitive income and expenses (NII) will change, impacting a bank's future financial result.
- Second, the present value and timing of future cash flows will change, resulting in changes of the underlying value of assets, liabilities, and off-balance sheet items, and hence a bank's economic value of equity (EVE).

Sound IRRBB management implies several steps. First, risk identification should be executed. Among all types of risks related to changes of interest rates those, which are relevant to the bank, should be chosen. For example, gap risk (comes from the term structure of banking book instruments), basis risk (arises when instruments with similar tenors are priced against different market reference rates/indices), yield curve risk (appears when the shape of the interest rate curve changes), are common to all banks. But optionality risk (arising from embedded in assets, liabilities, off-balance sheet items options, includes behavioral option risk) can be minor (or specific) in different banks.

As the next step, the identified risks should be measured in terms of their potential negative impact of prescribed interest rate shock scenarios[5] on capital, net interest income, and EVE. The economic value measures compute a change in the NPV of banks' assets, liabilities, and off-balance sheet items subject to specific interest rate shock and stress scenarios. They assess the effect of interest rate movements over the entire life of the balance sheet. The earnings-based measures focus on changes to future profitability within a given time horizon, usually the budgeting horizon of three to four years, and its further implications on banks' own funds. At this step special attention should be paid to treatment of non-standard positions, in particular, instruments with undefined maturities.

Finally, when amounts of potential negative impact are calculated, then a decision on which of them should be managed (which of them are not in line with the RAS) – should be taken. Risk management can be done by means of hedging with derivatives, equity investments, non-interest rate sensitive instruments, interest rate forecasting, and balance sheet planning. Capital adequacy for IRRBB must be specifically considered as part of the ICAAP.

To finalize, although the reason why ALM does not fit well any of the separate units (Risk, Trading Desk, or Finance) is unacceptable conflicts of interest arising, there are already well developed mechanisms that prevent conflict of interest at all working levels. First, this is the risk appetite statement and top-level metrics and restrictions mentioned in the beginning of this chapter. Second, the internal buffer/amber zones for risk appetite are set on subsequent collegial bodies (in particular, on the Asset and Liability Management Committee, ALCO, for ALM-related risks). The ALCO should obligatorily include representatives from ALM, Risk, and Finance. Business representatives are welcome to participate to be aware of current stance, limitations, tasks, or achievements, but not always have the voting right (and they definitely should be the minority of the members). This ensures decision-making with full awareness of the certain risks' consequences.

5 SPR 31.90–31.93 IRRBB, effective as of 15 Dec 2019, the Basel Framework, BIS, 2020.

Many measures have already been invented to resolve conflicts of interest, but it must be considered that conflicts of interest, including the ones in ALM, tend to intensify during periods of economic recession and crises, in conditions of increased uncertainty and the search for new ways to increase profitability. The solution to the conflict of interest is clearly defined rules regarding the functionality split, reporting lines and the place of ALM in the organizational structure of the bank. To avoid any conflict of interest, the ALM unit should be independent, give an unbiased assessment of the situation, be subordinate either to the CFO or CEO (when they have KPIs also on risk parameters), or within the unit responsible for the bank's long-term strategy. ALM should interact transparently with other departments of the bank and be supported by them. That means that Risk makes risk analysis reports (e.g., gap analysis) and provides them to the ALM. ALM analyzes these reports and makes conclusions (adding some more analysis – for example, the forecast of dynamics, based on the strategy and budget plan, provided to the ALM by Finance). Moreover, Finance provides calculations of the business units' results and ALM again makes conclusions – what to do to change (eliminate) negative trends impacts on the balance sheet. It can be realized by means of the Trading Desk, so ALM gives (approved by ALCO, of course) requests to the Trading Desk to make some hedging deals or to the business units to change their strategy (in volumes and rates). While analyzing the rates – ALM should consult the Trading Desk. Therefore, the ALM actively interacts with all banks' segments and makes managerial decisions based on their analytics and results.

Chapter 12
From a Standalone ALM Desk to a Group Treasury

A Group Treasury is the ALM desk for the whole banking group. That assumes that there is a head office and there are subsidiary banks – and as parts of a wider financial organization they have to interact with each other. There are no fixed rules for each Group Treasury. But according to the peculiarities of different cases (of different banking groups) there are specific models of Group Treasury, which are more recommended than the others.

First, before describing the models of Group Treasury – it is necessary to define the scope of tasks and problems that challenge Group Treasury. Some of the responsibilities are exactly the same as that of a standalone ALM desk, some of the responsibilities are the extensions of the latter.

Along with each ALM desk of a standalone bank, Group Treasury is responsible for ALM risk management and balance sheet structure targeting. The goals of Group Treasury in these aspects include the following:
- To ensure that regulatory and internal requirements (including Basel and individual SREP capital and liquidity requirements) of all the banks in the group and on the consolidated level are met.
- To analyze and manage interest rate and FX risk positions in the banking book (including minimization of risk position for hedgeable risks and precise control over non-hedgeable risks).
- To optimize liquidity buffer size and its composition in accordance with local specifics and yields of the local financial market.
- To ensure stable and cost-efficient funding for subsidiaries.
- To optimize capital consumption and capital adequacy ratios within the group and to ensure adequate capitalization within regulatory requirements and business plans.

Instead of income and resource allocation within business lines as a task of a standalone ALM desk – Group Treasury is responsible for implementation of group-wide methodologies of interest margin allocation within business lines, RWA allocation during budgeting and ad-hoc within subsidiaries and segments, proposals for dividend distribution portions, as well as group principles to ensure the comparability of values and results within different subsidiary banks.

And finally, instead of providing a benchmark for interest rates/prices to the business and settlement of the motivation system that a standalone ALM desk does, Group Treasury is responsible for designing FTP principles, models (and sometimes even curves themselves) in a way that optimizes usage of the bank's capital and liquidity and maximizes the group value.

https://doi.org/10.1515/9783110669763-015

These tasks of Group Treasury are challenged by key problems that each Group Treasury faces within its business, because of the geographical scale of business and differences of the banks within the group. Thus, each Group Treasury must deal with:

- *Different regulatory requirements on markets, where subsidiary banks operate.*

Every country usually has its own financial market/banking authority, which as a minimum translates world-known recommendations (e.g., Basel or EBA recommendations) into law, or if acting outside of the group of countries that follow such recommendations – introducing its own vision. The largest group of restrictions is represented by capital management indicators:

- Local lending limits define the maximum amount of exposure to one borrower/group of connected clients. From group management perspective it means that not all the subsidiaries will be able to equally participate in such deals as syndications of loans, trade finance deals, funded, and unfunded risk participations.
- Capital adequacy ratios and their components differ from bank to bank even within the same regulatory environment. If one speaks about different regulatory areas and regimes, then differences may occur even on a wider range of requirements. Inside one banking group the banks can be reporting to different regulators and, thus, the group and the local requirements may differ significantly.

Box 12.1. Decomposition of Regulatory Capital Requirements

In line with Basel III[1] recommendations, banks should differentiate three levels of capital: common equity tier 1 (CET1) capital, tier 1 (T1) capital, and total capital (see Figure 12.1).

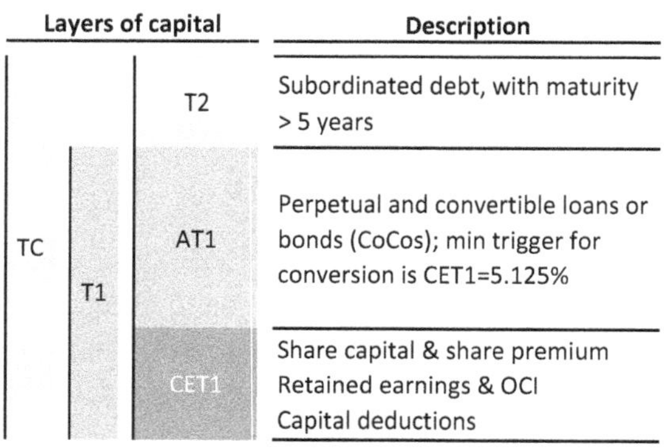

Figure 12.1: Layers of capital.

1 Basel III was implemented into the European Union law by Directive 2013/26/EU (CRD IV) and the CRR. Each EU country has implemented CRR and CRD IV into national laws amending the local Banking acts. In 2020–2021 a new banking package (Basel III.5) is coming into force with the introduction of CRD V, CRR II, and other regulations.

Common equity tier 1 capital consists of share capital and share premium, retained earnings, other comprehensive income and prudential filters/deductions, such as intangible assets, goodwill, deferred tax assets, etc.[2]

Tier 1 capital consists of CET1 capital and additional tier 1 (AT1) capital. Total capital consists of T1 capital and tier 2 (T2) capital. Both AT1 and T2 can be in the form of issued bonds or a loan. The main difference is that AT1 instruments should be perpetual, without defined maturity and should possess a trigger by reaching which instrument will be converted into CET1 capital. Regulatory defined trigger is CET1 capital ratio reaching a level of 5.125%, although many banks prefer to put the trigger higher. Of course, AT1 instrument is more expensive than T2, and it will require an even higher premium for subordination if the trigger is higher than the regulatory minimum.

T2 instruments may fail to be fully included in regulatory own funds because of the following reason: as the instrument reaches the date when it has less than five years until maturity the amortization starts and gradually comprises 20% each year, completely reaching 100% by maturity of the instrument. The amortized part is not included in the regulatory capital but can be considered as funding (so actual repayment does not take place) and MREL eligible liabilities (when residual maturity is not less than one year). It is important to note that only after reaching five years[3] from the date of issuance the T2 instrument can be called/redeemed/repaid or converted into AT1 or CET1 capital (approval from the regulatory authority is always necessary).

Capital requirements are, in general, imposed on the total own funds (total capital), but in some components can differentiate for different capital layers (see Figure 12.2). Basel III defines Pillar I requirements for each layer of capital: CET1 capital should not be less than 4.5% of total risk weighted assets, T1 capital – not less than 6% of RWA and total capital – not less than 8%, simultaneously.[4] Pillar I requirements represent the minimum common capital adequacy ratios that each bank should fulfill.

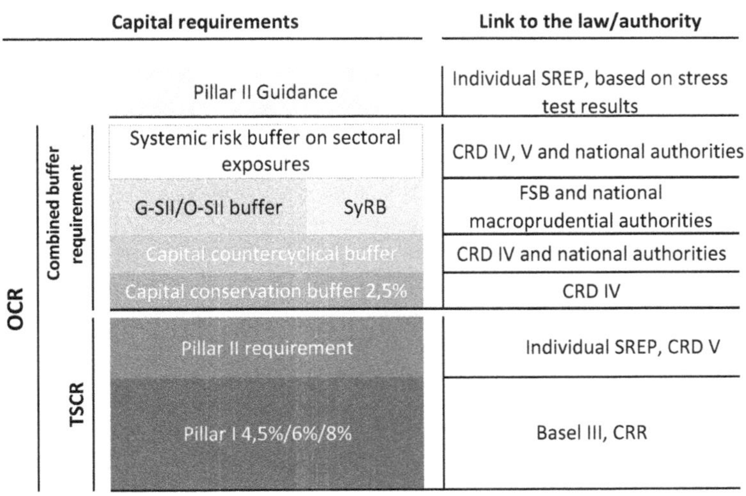

Figure 12.2: Capital requirements.

2 J. Ramirez, *Handbook Basel III Capital. Enhancing Bank Capital in Practice.* John Wiley & Sons, 2016.

3 Art. 63 CRR II.

4 Art. 92 CRR II.

The difference in capital adequacy requirements for different capital layers represents the only limitation for the components of regulatory own funds, whereas for purposes of large exposure management eligible capital has a limitation on T2 amount: it is included in calculation of eligible capital in the amount not exceeding one third of T1 capital.[5] With completion of CRR II implementation (by 28.06.2021) it is expected that eligible capital will no longer include T2 instruments for the purposes of large exposure management.

Another obligatory for fulfillment part of requirements is an individual add-on (Pillar II requirement) imposed as a result of SREP.[6] Following the principle of proportionality, these add-ons are usually applied only to the largest and the most important financial institutions operating in the markets that already introduced Basel III pillars.

Pillar I and Pillar II requirements form the Total SREP Capital Ratio (TSCR), which banks should fulfill at all times, including times of stress. Failure to fulfill TSCR would mean a failure of the bank when resolution mechanisms should start to take place.

Combined buffer requirements are implemented in addition to the capital requirements according to CRD IV (and their further amendments) and are meant to be drawn on by banks in periods of stress. There are currently three main types of capital buffers:

1) Capital conservation buffer – in line with CRD IV was fully phased-in by January 2019 in the amount of 2.5%.
2) Countercyclical capital buffer (CCyB) can be imposed by national supervisory authorities[7] and is calculated for the amount of exposure to borrowers based in countries with imposed CCyB (on the group level that would mean a weighted average on RWA buffer rate).
3) Systemic risk buffer (including Global (G-SII) and other (O-SII) systemically important institutions buffers) is implemented according to CRD IV and CRD V by Financial Stability Board (in respect to G-SII buffer) and by local macro-prudential authorities. If an institution is subject to systemic risk buffer (SyRB) and G-SII/O-SII, it must meet the higher of the two buffer requirements. According to CRD V (which was still not in place at the time of writing this chapter), the SyRB will be imposed to a specific subset of exposures, and not on the entire exposure of the bank. Its calculation will be similar to the calculation of the CCyB for a banking group.

Combined buffer requirements together with the TSCR make the overall capital ratio (OCR), which is the minimum capital requirement for banks in baseline (not stressed) conditions.

On top of OCR supervising authorities also impose Pillar II Guidance (P2G) as a result of individual SREP assessment and stress test of the bank. It is not obligatory, and breach of the P2G triggers only notification of the regulatory authorities with description of the reasons for this breach and a capital plan, showing how the recovery of the capital position to the level above P2G will take place. Nevertheless, all banks should aim to maintain P2G, in order to continue business as usual with dividend payments and other distributions.

---

5 Art. 4 (71) CRR II.

6 The Supervisory Review and Evaluation Process ("SREP") refers to the competent authorities' evaluation of the institution based on common methodologies and standards (see more in Chapter 13).

7 Information on currently applicable CCyB in different countries is published on European Systemic Risk Board website (https://www.esrb.europa.eu/national_policy/ccb/html/index.en.html), as well as on websites of local national banks.

On the 12th of March 2020 for the first time ever ECB provided temporary capital relief,[8] aiming to support banks to execute their function during the economic downturn because of the COVID-19 virus. All banks under ECB supervision were granted the right to temporary breach P2G and CCB. Almost all other local national banks followed ECB approach and allowed banks to temporarily steer capital below CCB and/or P2G because of losses due to the crisis. Most of the local supervisory authorities have lifted or significantly decreased CCyB requirements and canceled plans to increase it.

Another significant group is liquidity requirements, which also differ from country to country:
- LCR[9]/NSFR requirements through local introduction can be applied in different countries with differences in calculations. In some countries, local requirements (e.g., on survival horizon) can be stricter than the internationally accepted ratios LCR/NSFR.
- Liquidity buffer requirements in terms of percentage of total assets, as well as in terms of decomposition of the buffer.
- Specific constraints to transfer funds (portfolios) across legal entities and jurisdictions. For example, national authorities aiming to protect domestic customers may prevent transferring retail loans abroad.

To this category one can also add decisions of the local management boards on the internal buffers and indicators of the Risk Appetite Statement.

As a result of regulatory differences, a task of optimization of funding and capital consumption across the group becomes more complicated for the Group Treasury. This task becomes even more vital in times of economic slowdown: reduced availability of liquidity and capital makes strategic pricing/internal pricing and resource planning (funding/capital) more important.

- *Local specifics of markets influencing on the size of subsidiaries, their growth rate, types of business lines, and product parameters.*

This group of limitations can be split into quantitative and qualitative ones.

The quantitative peculiarities and differences may be described by level of interest rates, their volatility, level of uncertainty in the overall banking environment, stability of exchange rates, etc. Following specific set of quantitative parameters, a bank would need different instruments and measures to close the maturity or currency mismatch to hedge the interest rate and FX risk; the costs of funding, strategic RoE, and allocation will be also impacted.

8 https://www.bankingsupervision.europa.eu/press/pr/date/2020/html/ssm.pr200312~43351ac3ac.en.html

9 In 2020 in line with capital requirements reliefs due to the COVID-19 crisis, ECB, and some local competent authorities allowed banks to operate below the level of LCR.

Product mix and market dynamics can be also considered as quantitative specifics. Availability (or lack) of different bank products offered to clients, instruments and/or funding maturities form the balance sheet structure and determine the challenges ALM would have to cope with. For example, if the banking market offers only saving accounts for its customers – for the balance sheet this would mean a task to assess the stickiness of funds and to split the undefined maturity accounts into proper time buckets. Another situation would be if there's a high uncertainty in the market – and, thus, the maximum available tenor of funding would be one year for financing of long-term assets (like mortgage loans). This would require involvement of IRSs (often together with FX derivatives) to hedge IRR. Differences on the assets side, such as offering a simple loan or lending with embedded options, derivatives, insurance, and other bonuses for the customer requires different pricing models.

The qualitative part of limitations includes customers' behavioral patterns and cultural peculiarities in every particular country. For example, if the customers do not trust in banks, due to the experiences of many banking turbulences in the past – no product offers would immediately change this behavior. The retail customers will continue to run the banks each time when they hear any controversial news or even rumors. One more example is when some country may have oligopoly of several banks, making development for a bank outside this narrow circle of trust much more difficult. This oligopoly may be even supported (if not promoted) by the state and the customers will, of course, choose more secured banks with the state support.

Another qualitative peculiarity may be because of how people have been doing business for ages. For example, the process of negotiations may be executed in a direct or indirect manner. The bank may agree to have a good client with less plausible conditions and neglect the best practice in pricing (thinking that good relations with a customer sometimes are more valuable than a positive margin of the deal).

The ability (or its absence) of subsidiaries to make deals on local markets in different currencies and for different tenors, the scale effect in different interest rate environments form structural liquidity, interest rate and FX risks contribution to financial result of the subsidiary and of the group. These balance sheet risks of different sources and complexity must be managed by the Group Treasury. This task becomes even more complicated if a subsidiary bank operates in markets where it is unable to hedge all the risks.

- *Double reporting lines within a group from subsidiaries to local heads and head office* may cause conflicts or ambiguity.

The usual situation in banking groups is that each banking area, and the ALM/ Treasury as well, has its supervisor (or at least a contact person) in the head office. Line managers have a possibility to address questions to that supervisor and must provide requested information for the group consolidation. Cooperation with this supervisor may go further beyond periodic reporting when the head office requests ad-hoc analysis and calculations. Here comes space for ambiguity, as the assumptions from the head office may differ from the assumptions of the direct manager from the local bank. For example, the head office may want to get a calculation of impacts of business lines or a branch winding down on capital and liquidity, whereas the local management does not consider such a scenario at all! In this case the line managers and experts are subject to a difficult choice – whose instructions and assumptions to apply. Luckily in many jurisdictions[10] in these situations local managers are supported by the supervisors from regulatory competent authories, who control that there's no external significant influence on local decision-making.

Also reporting of the same categories, but in different formats – for local reporting and for the group needs – double the work and efforts, when not automated.

To prevent these problems, proper establishment of the structure and governance within the group becomes an important task for the Group Treasury. This task is easier if strong central liquidity management framework and group oversight is required by the home regulator. In other cases, the Group Treasury must make a choice between the available operational models.

There are two basic operational models for Group Treasury: centralized and decentralized. Naturally, a mixture of centralized and decentralized models gives life to many models, as each time the mixture is different according to the needs of the group. Below the description of each basic model is given, followed by arguments for the model choice in accordance with the type of banking group and factors accompanying its activities.

Centralized Group Treasury model is characterized by strong dependence of subsidiaries' Internal Treasuries/ALM desks on the Group Treasury. All the interaction between different subsidiaries (if needed) is executed through the head office. There is a clear Group strategy, defined in the head office and applicable to all the subsidiaries, followed by strict group standards, templates, and limits. It finds its application first in governance and then in practical issues.

Centralized governance requires that subsidiaries Internal Treasuries' organizational structure completely reflects one of the head offices. Subsidiaries have the same structural units as the Group Treasury (operational liquidity, FTP and resource allocation, strategic IRR and banking book management, capital adequacy management, etc.) and report to the latter within each unit. Group Treasury has direct influence on subsidiary Treasuries' action plans, budget, amount of staff, even takes part in hiring/firing decisions for subsidiary Internal Treasuries' staff, and defines KPIs for heads of structural units of subsidiaries' ALM desk.

---

10 Guidelines on internal governance under Directive 2013/36/EU, EBA/GL/2017/11, EBA, 26 September 2017; Joint ESMA and EBA Guidelines on the assessment of the suitability of members of the management body and key function holders under Directive 2013/36/EU and Directive 2014/65/EU, EBA/GL/2017/12, ESMA and EBA, 26 September 2017.

Group Treasury determines policies and rolls out methodology to subsidiaries. Subsidiaries align the group principles and methodology with their operating procedures, although all the adjustments and amendments must be approved by the Group Treasury. Within centralized governance Group Treasury defines all the reports for subsidiaries to be provided. These reports are obligatory to subsidiaries in addition to reporting to local supervisory authority.

Group Treasury ensures availability to subsidiaries of funding and acts as the primary lender for them. Subsidiaries can raise funds in financial market only in local currencies (of the country where a subsidiary operates) and in line with the funding plan developed by the Group Treasury.

Capital position is also controlled by the Group Treasury (according to the plan of optimal capital allocation among the subsidiaries). Excessive capital is withdrawn by the group in the form of dividends (as part of the previous year's profit or from retained earnings), capital shortfall is covered by capital injections only after alignment of the capital measure on the group level. Subsidiaries' appetite for risk should be in line with the capitalization plan of the group, only top-down decisions about capital can be made. The only responsibility of subsidiaries' Internal Treasuries is compliance with local regulations (due to their better local expertise and interaction with local competent authorities).

Box 12.2. Optimization of the Group Capital Structure

As it was described earlier, CET1 is the most expensive type of capital for the head office (which within a banking group is acting as investor). At the same time, regulation (in particular, in the form of CRR) prescribes to comply with capital adequacy requirements (to cover capital need) with different quality of own funds. Amendment to CRD IV (CRD V introduction) enabled even higher share of lower quality own funds by imposing differentiation of P2R on different capital layers (P2R should be covered by CET1 at least in amount of 56.25% and by T1 in amount of at least 75%).

Many subsidiary banks, as a heritage from the past – before the regulation amendments, may have that high level of CET1 capital, that would cover Pillar I and Pillar II requirements in full, what represent from the head office point of view higher than necessary CET1 capital amount. By optimizing capital structure in the subsidiaries by means of utilization up to the maximum eligible levels of AT1 and T2 a group can:

- Save tax expenses (it happens, while paying interest on subordinated loans subsidiaries would decrease their tax base).
- Increase RoE of subsidiary banks and head office solo, and increase by that investment attractiveness of the banks (withdrawing dividends would decrease the equity of subsidiaries and the ratio of RoE would increase; the head office would increase its profits by getting the dividends and also interest from subsidiaries and the RoE ratio would also increase).
- Improve group market value and avoid losses regarding sale of subsidiaries below its book value (usually M&A deals consider subordinated loans without discounts, and the price of the deal is only opposed to the net asset value, in other words the equity, of a bank).

In practice it can be achieved in the following steps, triggered by the head office:

1) Assessment of the maximum number of dividends, which can be paid out by subsidiaries
   a. At the first moment, the capital surplus to CET1 capital requirement should be considered. If the surplus is significant, it should be checked if the bank has legal capacity to pay-out this amount.
   b. The dividend payout capacity is determined by distributable items[11] (Art 4 para 1 no 128 CRR) – see Table 12.1.

Table 12.1: Distributable items of own funds.

Distributable items
+ profits at the end of the last financial year
+ profits brought forward
+ reserves available for distribution
- losses brought forward
- profits that are non-distributable (according to law or by-laws)
- sums placed to non-distributable reserves (according to law or statutes)
= distributable items

In general, it is possible to take dividends only if the subsidiary has accumulated a positive result (last year's profit or positive retained earnings over the years). If a subsidiary bank has negative retained earnings, they should be neutralized (by reclassification from share capital into retained earnings, subject to regulatory approval) to create availability to pay-out generated profit as dividends in the following years. According to the CRR, the reduction of CET1 items by payout of dividends does not require an approval by the competent authority. During this step it is necessary to check the tax issues with regard to dividends payout: if there's a withholding tax, if it is limited by the Double Tax Treaty, or if there's a Parent-Subsidiary-Directive, which stipulates that cross-border dividend payments between companies on qualified shareholdings stay free of withholding taxes.

2) Request of dividend payments from available own funds reserves, defined in Step 1.
3) Verification of T1 capital and total capital shortfalls to regulatory requirements in order to ensure the strategic business growth.

T2 and AT1 instruments should be provided to subsidiaries in amounts up to the maximal amount still eligible as own funds (that corresponds to (2%+0.25%*P2R) of RWA for T2 instruments and to (1.5% + 0.1875*P2R) of RWA for AT1 instruments; of course, if some other buffers/requirements diversify for different layers of capital – it should also be taken into account). In first line T2 subordinated loans should be provided to the maximal extent due to their lower interest and only after T2 capacity is used, then AT1 instruments should be provided. In total, new T2 and AT1 provided should amount to no more than CET1, which is planned to be withdrawn. This will ensure pure optimization of the capital structure.

11 Art. 4 (1/128) CRR.

During this step it is necessary to check the tax issues again, in particular with regard to hybrid AT1 instruments: in some jurisdictions interest expense on AT1 instruments is treated as dividends, thus, not deductible from the tax base and may trigger a withholding tax (as in Step 1).

4) After this one-off substitution is done, the strategy for the next years will be further injections of lower level capital to subsidiaries in line with the growth of their RWA (the more RWA, the more T2 and AT1 can be given, according to the formula mentioned in Step 3).

Simultaneously, ambitious dividend distribution plan should be in place, aiming by payouts of the previous year's profit to compensate for capital injected.

From the scope of practical issues subsidiaries manage local portfolios according to the group guidelines for interest rate and FX risk management and defined by Group Treasury limits. Group Treasury has the right to monitor execution of deals and their alignment with group standards. This concerns not only the deals of local Internal Treasuries, but also the deals of the local business, which impact the whole group's financial result. Here the Group Treasury controls the alignment of accomplished deals within the centrally developed FTP principles and consistency of application of these principles during the whole deal making process (from the moment of deal construction until the moment of reflection of results in the local managerial system).

The centralized Group Treasury model is valuable for providing transparency and comparability of the results of all the entities within the banking group, as well as for reducing costs for the group due to scale effect and optimizing deals structuring and coordination due to acting as the only counterparty in the market. The major drawback of this model is that centralized funding and capital allocation can not be the cheapest option due to neglected economic cost differentials between legal entities, as well as centrally developed methodologies can fail to take into account local specifics of subsidiary banks.

Decentralized Group Treasury model is characterized by high independence of subsidiaries from the head office. Interaction of subsidiaries with other banks in the group is accomplished according to the local needs and understanding of the markets by local management. Subsidiaries' Internal Treasuries report directly only to their CFOs/CEOs and not to the Group Treasury. Only high-level group guidelines are issued and according to these guidelines local decision-making and execution takes place in practice.

From the managerial point of view subsidiaries' Internal Treasuries are separated and independent from the Group Treasury and may have quite different organizational structures from the one in head office. Group Treasury may ask subsidiaries to provide only high-level reports to the head office; all other reporting is executed locally for local decisive bodies.

Group Treasury has no influence on subsidiaries' ALM desk action plan, budget or staff amount. Group Treasury defines only a number of high-level (and crucial for the banking group) KPIs on liquidity and capital to local CEO, who translates them into operational KPIs at local ALM desk level. As a rule, Group Treasury is not involved in hiring/firing process of subsidiaries ALM desk's staff and may only possess a voting right with regards to subsidiaries' heads of Internal Treasuries.

Group defines high-level group methodology, providing space and freedom to subsidiaries to implement their independent policies in line with the group standards. Responsibility for compliance with local regulations, determination of risk appetite level as well as capital allocation to different risks or business lines naturally remains within subsidiaries.

Subsidiaries are responsible for all funding in all currencies they may need. The Group Treasury reviews and approves subsidiaries' funding plans and incorporates into group plan and acts as the lender of last resort only in cases of emergency. Subsidiaries are also allowed to issue their own debt, including capital; the Group Treasury coordinates the process of capital issuance, provides its expertise in this question and can facilitate the communication with market participants.

From the practical aspect the Group Treasury defines country limits (including the limits for interest rate and FX risks), with which subsidiaries are required to comply while managing local portfolios. Subsidiaries define their own set of detailed limits. The same is true for FTP and pricing methodology: high-level guidelines are given by the Group Treasury although the subsidiaries develop their own methodology according to the local specifics, calculate locally, and only notify the Group Treasury about the applied principles.

The decentralized Group Treasury model has the main advantage of accounting of all the local specifics of the environment, where subsidiary banks operate. Although this model requires high competences at each local level, what is not always possible and definitely more expensive for the whole banking group (as not only the head office staff should be highly educated and experienced, but also all the local ones). Furthermore, lack of scale shortens the list of possible funding sources and hedging instruments – which will also increase the costs. Moreover, independence of the subsidiaries may cause a problem of clients' arbitrage against the banking group due to the lack of transparency and control within this model.

Both models for the Group Treasury – centralized and decentralized have their virtues and drawbacks, although sometimes there are definite external and internal factors and criteria, which determine the choice. They are the following.

Specific regulatory requirements across markets. If local regulator requires only local ALM desk to be responsible for asset and liability management and resources allocation – then this is an argument toward the decentralized model, and the Group Treasury would have to act as the high-level supervisor.

Geographical spread of banking business and local peculiarities (geographical and cultural factor). When the activities of the banking group are concentrated in the same region (e.g., in different countries of Western Europe) with approximately the same level of living and business traditions – then there's no need to double treasury functions by implementing the decentralized operating model. Awareness about local specifics starts to play a huge role in defining the better model for a group with presence in different world areas. Alignment of subsidiary's ALM desk with local business and understanding the market environment provides advantage to the subsidiary's ALM desk in comparison to the Group Treasury, which obviously can't have full information being based in a different country. Consequently, in this case the decentralized model is preferable.

Local markets' development level. Lack of financial instruments, little access to financial markets, undeveloped markets and financial relations will lead a subsidiary, operating in these circumstances, to shortage (or lack) of funding and capital resources (senior/subordinated debt) in financial markets. This will cause high dependence of this subsidiary on the head office in terms of fundraising, liquidity, and capital issues. In this case application of the centralized model is essential.

The level of expertise of the Group Treasury and its ability to operate in environment with diverse and unconnected systems (not integrated IT systems) also determines the type of the model for the Group Treasury. Centralized model will increase the group's value only if the Group Treasury has enough experience, skills, and capabilities to understand local market and local business requirements.

The type and diversification of business (specialization of the banking group). If the banking group is large and its business mix is focused mainly on commercial banking, then expectedly clients are coming from geographical clusters (from main financial centers of the world). Therefore, the banking group needs to accumulate the most knowledge and more skilled talents, as well as independence in those "hubs" (with the main "hub" in the city, where the largest cluster is based) and other subsidiaries can be managed from the "hub" or by the Group Treasury. This example represents the idea of the mixture of the Group Treasury operating models. The same is true, when the relative size of the head office and among the subsidiaries significantly differ: one large domestic market and small foreign ones (or several "hubs" in the world financial centers) force to allocate all the power to the Group Treasury (or to the head office and "hubs" within a mixture of models).

After the 2007–2008 crisis there was a rush toward centralization of treasuries, while also technological advances and solutions for asset and liability management made it easier. Nevertheless in line with regulatory amendments some advantages of the centralized Group Treasury model disappeared, making this model not the best one to apply. Of course, still some groups can be considered as examples of the pure centralized or decentralized operating model. For example, Lloyds banking group according to its International markets' key activities[12] can be prone to have the centralized operating model. Santander group, on the contrary, emphasizes that its business model is based on local, legally independent, and autonomous

12 www.lloyds.com/internationalmarkets

entities in terms of capital and liquidity,[13] what means preferring the decentralized Group Treasury operating model.

Although recent trends in banking business force large banking groups to implement a mixture of the basic operating models. Increased risk awareness makes central banks impose harder regulatory requirements. As an effect of globalization, the rules and constraints across countries tend to differentiate less from country to country. For example, the Dodd-Frank Act in the United States and European Market Infrastructure Regulation (EMIR) in European Union are meant to impose similar regulatory constraints, although they have differences in product scope and require different reporting. Moreover, local central banks highlight the importance of sustainability of each local bank (a subsidiary in a banking group) by ring-fencing of capital and funding along regional lines. The Basel recommendations towards capital solvency[14] make it more costly to provide capital to subsidiaries and thus leading some banking groups to a decision of subsidiaries' independence in questions of capital and long-term funding, only optimizing centrally the use of resources in order to avoid unwanted risk-taking across the group.

The new banking package (Basel III.5) requests for non-European banking groups, which have more than one significant subsidiary in the European Union, to establish an "Intermediate EU parent," which would be responsible for EU subsidiaries operations.[15]

The combination always provides flexibility and is meant to achieve required optimal group structure (by choosing the optimal model for each structural unit), but there are also some side effects of hybrid model application. Due to matrix structure (with double reporting lines) the model becomes more complex, less transparent and rather difficult to govern it with a need to build strong control framework over "independent" subsidiaries' Internal Treasuries.

To finalize, no matter which Group Treasury model or mix of the two basic ones the banking group will choose – its principles, rules, and responsibility allocation (what tasks and to what extent are responsible for one or another unit of the banking group) should be clearly defined and well understood by everybody – both, in the Group Treasury and in subsidiaries' Internal Treasuries.

---

13 www.santander.com

14 Basel III: A global regulatory framework for more resilient banks and banking systems//BIS December 2010 (rev June 2011).

15 Art. 21b CRD V. The criteria for necessity of the Intermediate EU parent are 2 and more subsidiaries of the same third-country banking group with cumulative value of total assets more than 40 bn EUR. This regulation is planned to become obligatory beginning 30 December 2023.

Conclusions

ALM tasks, responsibilities, methodologies, and outcomes are applicable to all balance sheet items, are interconnected with the majority of other departments in a bank and widely support the management board decision-making in achieving banks' long-term goals.

By proper settlement of an ALM operating model (in a stand-alone bank and in a banking group) ALM avoids conflicts of interest with other participants of the balance sheet risk-management triangle, which are the Risk Department, Finance and External Treasury-Trading Desk. ALM should be an independent function from either of the three but interact and inform each of them daily (also within the lines of defense). Introducing either of the target Treasury operating models (the front office Treasury or the middle office Treasury) – ALM can fulfill a more operational or a more strategic function, although by any of both preserving banks' capital, liquidity, and the balance sheet overall.

By choosing an optimal Group Treasury model (the centralized, decentralized, or mixed (hybrid) Group Treasury), ALM can address strengths, opportunities, and general peculiarities of the banking group. A proper Group Treasury structure helps to optimize capital and funding, resources consumption within the group, avoid clients' arbitrage, and optimize operational expenses for the Group Treasury function.

https://doi.org/10.1515/9783110669763-016

Part 3: New Trends in Banking and Challenges for ALM

It is always difficult to predict the future. At the same time, when banks can anticipate further challenges – they will be able to prepare themselves for periods of turbulences.

By 2020–2021 the regulatory uncertainty was planned to come to its end with completion of the reform process. Banking reforms tend to increase proportionality of application of rules and laws, address particularly more risks, cover even potential losses with capital and funds. ALM, responsible for steering these scarce resources and having a holistic picture of the bank's stance and development, starts to be involved in almost all processes in a bank. Specifics of the banking business (small solo-bank, or large banking group; operating on a developed market or catching up on the trends in an emerging economy) impacts ALM activities.

Developing markets will be following best practice of the developed economies, small banks will have reliefs on some tasks in comparison to large banking groups. The new challenges will face mainly large banks on developed markets.

The preplanned development of banking regulations was frozen for a while by the COVID-19 crisis that stopped economies worldwide for several months. Recovery from this complete lock-down would require years for best economies of the world, and decades for developing markets. As this crisis was not driven by undervaluing of some financial risks, the processes of how to react to the crisis were already in place for major of countries and banks. Although, the financial world did not yet have a chance to experience that scale of a downturn and had to learn one more lesson. ALM was not an exception. Moreover, ALM was the most important department at the start of the crisis and contributed to the usual banking activities as well as in the crisis ad-hoc requests. To understand the additional tension on ALM in the crisis, one first should figure out, what the usual role of ALM was in the bank's steering.

This part of the book covers the following questions:

- How deep is ALM involved in banks' processes and how does it impact the future stance of the bank?
- Is ALM role in banks of different scale and background the same or different?
- What additional tasks appear for ALM in periods of crises?
- What signals of future changes in the ALM area can already be observed?

https://doi.org/10.1515/9783110669763-017

Chapter 13
ALM Role in SREP

In general, Supervisory Review and Evaluation Process (SREP) is a mechanism imposed in Pillar II of Basel III to ensure that banks have sufficient capital to support all the risks associated with their businesses. Thus, SREP is an ongoing supervisory process bringing together findings from all supervisory activities performed on an institution into a comprehensive supervisory overview. As a result of SREP each supervised bank receives a score and individual capital requirement add-on (the Pillar-2 Requirement, P2R). The score is based on scores in four areas of assessment, although does not follow any particular mathematical dependency. The four areas are:

A) Business model analysis (whether the business model of the bank can ensure sustainable growth of the institution, even in times of market downturns).
B) Internal governance and institution-wide controls (whether the management processes are transparent, decision-making process is independent and based on all sufficient information about risks and environment).
C) Risks to capital (whether capital steering is in line with the latest regulatory requirements, the quantity of risk is sufficiently covered by the own funds at the current moment and on the planning horizon).
D) Risks to liquidity and funding (whether liquidity steering is in line with the latest regulatory requirements, there are stable and sustainable sources of funding at the current moment and on the planning horizon).

As a result of SREP other than P2R quantitative and qualitative capital, liquidity and other measures can be imposed on the bank.

ALM takes part in representing each of the areas, to a larger or smaller extent, and is impacted by the results of the assessment.

Box 13.1. Main Principles of SREP

SREP is based on the following main principles, which are used by supervisory authorities in evaluation of different banks across European countries:

- Principle of proportionality
- Principle of consistency (of methodologies for the assessment of capital and liquidity adequacy)
- Common, uniform, and consistent application of European Union law (Directive 2013/36/EU)
- Principle of continuity of risk assessment
- Efficient and effective supervisory practices

Following principle of proportionality all financial institutions are categorized in four distinct categories according to their importance to the global or a local financial system and the extent of any cross-border activities. Institutions are characterized by:

- Size
- Structure
- Internal organization

https://doi.org/10.1515/9783110669763-018

- Scope of business
- Nature and complexity of activities
- Level of systemic risk posed by an institution

As a result, global systemically important institutions (G-SIIs) and other systemically important institutions (O-SIIs) and other institutions determined by competent authorities constitute Category 1. Category 2 consists of non-systemically important specialized institutions with significant market shares in their lines of business or payment systems, or financial exchanges. To Category 3 specialized institutions with less significant market shares in their lines of business or payment systems, or financial exchanges are added. Category 4 includes all other small non-complex domestic institutions that do not fall into other categories. Depending on the category of the institution the depth, intensity, and frequency of assessments are varied.

Principle of consistency means that key indicators are monitored:
- Financial and risk indicators addressing all risk categories
- All the ratios derived from the application of CRR and CRD IV (with their further amendments) for calculating the minimum prudential requirements (e.g., Core Equity Tier 1, LCR, NSFR, etc.)
- MREL
- Relevant market-based indicators (e.g., equity price, credit default swap (CDS) spreads, bond spreads, etc.)
- Recovery indicators used in the institution's own recovery plans
- Identification of material changes or anomalies in indicators

Principle of continuity of risk assessment deals with frequency and periodicity of assessments. In line with this principle supervisory authorities:
- Monitor key indicators on a quarterly basis (may establish more frequent monitoring)
- Produce a documented summary of the overall SREP assessment at least annually
- Update the assessments of all individual SREP elements at least annually
- Inform the institution of the outcome of the overall SREP assessment at least annually by issuing the following documents:
  - A statement on the quantity and composition of the own funds the institution is required to hold in excess of the requirements specified in CRR and CRD IV (and their further amendments).
  - A statement on the liquidity held and any specific liquidity requirements.
  - A statement on other supervisory measures, including any early intervention measures.

All supervisory best practices are described in the SREP Guidelines,[1] based on which all supervisory reviews are executed.

During the *Business model* analysis supervisory authorities consider the following topics:
- Ability to generate acceptable returns over the following 12 months and over a forward-looking period of at least three years. ALM is responsible for the following parts of this topic:
  - Capital and funding planning (with defining amounts, tenors, and rates of raised funds)

1 Guidelines on common procedures and methodologies for the supervisory review and evaluation process (SREP) and supervisory stress testing, EBA/GL/2014/13, 19 July 2018.

  - Maturity transformation steering (by either hedging the IRR, or changing the balance sheet structure)
  - Determination of pricing models, targeting client pricing
  - Defining CoC and taking part in proposal of strategic RoE for the bank (by calculation CAPM models and/or making market peer-group comparison)
- Analysis of the current business model, forward-looking strategy, and financial plans are not possible without consideration of funding and capital plans, as well as recovery and resolution plans – where again ALM is one of the main characters inside the bank.
- Business environment is assessed by defining of the material/critical business lines and services of the bank, as well as the peer-group. ALM is not among these services (as only the ones for external customers (which represent part of financial system) are considered). ALM plays mainly a role of the user of this information – in other topics, like strategic RoE definition and/or defending its position with regard to resolution topic.
- In part of identification of the institution's key vulnerabilities, which are most likely to have a material impact on the institution/lead to its failure in the future – ALM may be invited to take part in regulatory dialog and defend some of the weaker areas of the bank by giving examples of successful solving of some of the issues.

The conclusion here is that ALM should participate in all the meetings with regard to discussion of *business model* and present its view on banks' development and available solutions for vulnerable situations.

Assessment of *internal governance and institution-wide controls* deals with a wider and a more detailed spectrum of topics, as such:

- Overall internal governance framework, whether
  - Organizational structure is transparent and with clear responsibilities.
  - The management body knows and understands operational structure.
  - Policies avoid conflicts of interest, outsourcing policies meet regulatory requirements.
  - Internal governance framework is transparent to stakeholders.

As described in Part 2, ALM can be involved in several conflicts of interest, and it is also its role and responsibility to avoid those conflicts – in this part ALM contributes to overall governance framework. Also, ALM should explicitly inform management about development of liquidity, capital, also new regulatory requirements and need for measures to steer these components. ALM is needed to start the management discussion about these particularly important topics, raising controversial topics, which require management acknowledgment and decision.

- Corporate and risk culture, whether
  - The management body bears main responsibility for the institution, sets governance principles, corporate values, clear and strong communication of strategies, and policies to all relevant staff.

Here supervisors investigate, if decisions are made in line with the approved strategy and whether all parts of the organization understand it. ALM is very much dependent on strategy, and only its deep understanding would allow ALM to offer the management appropriate steering measures, as well as proper inputs for business planning.
  - The management body is independent, fit, and proper; internal control framework (internal audit function) has clear allocation of responsibilities; remuneration policies and practices are aligned with banks' risk appetite.
- Risk management framework, including ICAAP and ILAAP, whether it has a link to the risk appetite framework, strategic plan, capital, and liquidity management frameworks.

  This is the part of internal governance topics, which is most of all impacted by ALM. ALM's role here is to implement all regulatory requirements into the steering framework and to reflect in a subsequent manner in group policies. By means of regulatory dialogs, consultation papers and Q&As with banking supervisors ALM must understand, correctly describe in policies and implement in practice, what exactly is being required within every single topic of regulatory interest.
- Information systems and business continuity, whether up-to-date risk data are available in a timely manner; recovery planning arrangements are in place.

  An example of ALM contribution will be timely available forecasts and planning of capital and liquidity on different time horizons and in different scenarios. An adverse scenario for a bank would lead to recovery indicators breach and triggering recovery measures to restore capital, liquidity, and profitability.

Regulators and banks believe that governance topics are of the most importance in the SREP process. Although individual SREP scores are disclosed neither by banks, nor by the supervisors, there is some evidence to conclude, that there is no bank in the world that has the best available score ("1" of 4) for this SREP part.

ALM role is not leading in this topic, nonetheless, is extremely crucial. ALM is one of the functions that form the basement of the proper functioning of the organization, awareness of the management, and prudent decision-making process. Every ALM manager should have a wider look on what ALM can contribute to the bank, aiming not only at achieving goals in its specific tasks, but also choosing the topics, working on which improvement can bring the whole bank on a different level.

The next two areas of SREP are unattainably connected with ALM.

In *Risks to capital* area regulators are concerned about the following:
- Inherent individual risk (split into credit, market, operational, and IRRBB risks). Scope of assessment includes nature and composition of credit/market portfolios, concentration of risk, profitability of portfolio and set targets, risk-adjusted performance of the portfolio, own funds requirement for risk compared to the total own funds requirement, stress testing results.

There is not much ALM can do with the credit, market, or operational risk. It is very much dependent on the overall strategy and risk model of the bank. For example, if a bank was to invest all its funds into government risk-free bonds – it would show a perfect credit and market risk picture, but such a strategy won't pay-off for any commercial institution. On the contrary, IRRBB is in responsibility of ALM (see Box 11.2) – and proper policies and models should prove sustainability of the bank.

- Risk management and controls. Scope of assessment includes credit risk strategy and appetite; organizational framework; policies and procedures; risk identification, measurement, monitoring, and reporting; internal control framework.

  It can be noticed that there is an interception with the previous section of the regulatory assessment process. This is not a coincidence: SREP intends to check and cross-check all the areas, finding interrelation of topics and getting confirmation that the same risk management approach is applied through the bank.

Box 13.2. Determination of P2R and P2G

As a result of SREP, banks under the single supervisory mechanism (SSM) receive an individual score and quantitative assessment of additional capital requirements (P2R and P2G, if applicable for the bank). Place of P2R and P2G in the stacking order of capital requirements and its interception with other capital requirement add-ons is described in Box 12.1.

P2R is defined based on the assessment of the whole bank, although information received in part of evaluation of risks to capital plays the most important role in quantification process. Regulator defines the following steps for determination of the P2R add-on.

1) Determination of the additional own funds' requirements on a risk-by-risk basis using internal quantifications of the bank (ICAAP calculations) is the starting point.

   For most of the banks P2R is not defined one-to-one as in ICAAP, because regulators do not find them reliable (see Table 13.1), and risk-specific supervisory benchmarks to account for business-model-specific considerations are then used.

Table 13.1: Criteria of ICAAP calculations reliability.

Criteria of ICAAP calculations reliability			
Granularity	**Credibility**	**Understandability**	**Comparability**
Calculations are broken down by risk type	Calculations reflect actual correlations and portfolio compositions; based on recognized or appropriate models and prudent assumptions	Underlying drivers of the calculations/ methodologies are clearly specified	Calculations facilitate comparability with peers and supervisory benchmark estimations

The rationale and general underlying principles behind the benchmarks should be explained to the institution, but can't be assessed by the bank in advance (and, thus, can't be implemented in budgeting and forecasting process; for budgeting and forecasting only conservative considerations on P2R level should be included).

2) Reconciliation of additional own funds requirements with the CRD buffers and any macro-prudential requirements.

   At this stage the competent authorities should check that the same risk isn't already covered by other specific capital buffer requirements and/or additional macro-prudential add-ons.
3) Determination of the TSCR ratio.

   At first, the Total SREP Capital Requirement in absolute volume is determined, as a result of steps 1 and 2. Then TSCR ratio is defined according to the formula: $TSCR\ ratio = 8\%* \frac{total\ SREP\ capital\ requirement*12.5}{total\ risk\ exposure\ amount}$. As already described in Box 12.1 TSCR = Pillar I requirement + Pillar II requirement. P2R should be covered at least in part of 56.25% by CET1 and at least in part of 75% by T1 capital (according to pre-loaded in 2020 CRD V principles).[2]

Based on assessment, whether the OCR and TSCR can be met over the economic cycle and in the stressed conditions, the P2G ratio is defined.

P2G means the level and quality of own funds the institution is expected to hold in excess of its OCR, determined based on stress test impact (see Figure 13.1). When determining P2G competent authorities:

A) ensure that it covers at least the anticipated maximum stress impact (based on the changes in the CET1 ratio in adverse scenarios) cumulatively in all years of stress

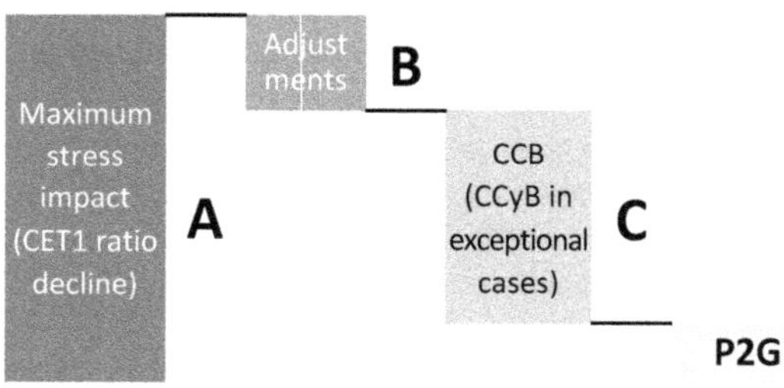

Figure 13.1: Definition of P2G.

B) consider the outcome of a reliable ICAAP stress test, the quality (and composition) of institution's available own funds. Relevant mitigating actions (e.g., additional capital injections, planned in the capital budget, but not signed yet by the parties) can be potentially considered during the next SREP process (e.g., in a year, for institutions under SSM).
C) consider how combined buffer requirements already cover risks revealed by stress testing: offset P2G against the capital conservation buffer and on a case-by-case basis against the capital contra-cyclical buffer. P2G is not offset against the systemic risk buffers, as those are intended to cover the risks an institution poses to the financial system.

In *Risks to liquidity and funding* area regulators are concerned about the following:

- Inherent liquidity risk (intraday, in the short and medium term, under normal and stressed conditions, in different currencies). It includes evaluation of liquidity buffer and counterbalancing capacity, its sustainability over time and in crisis

2 Art. 104a (4) CRD V.

situations (availability of the market access, development of the haircuts for the unencumbered assets in the liquidity buffer portfolio, committed, and not disbursed liquidity facilities).

As ALM is responsible for liquidity buffer management, it possesses the abovementioned information, although it would be more prudent if this information is provided to the regulator by the risk controlling function. Maintenance of market access at all times is in responsibilities of department responsible for interaction with financial institutions, while ALM only uses it for managing liquidity on a daily basis in a timely manner.

- Inherent funding risk, in particular banks' funding profile and its stability. It includes dependence on specific sources of funding, structural maturity mismatch, expected change in funding risk based on the institution's funding plan.

  Of course, ALM contributes a lot to elaboration of the funding strategy and decomposition of different funding types. Depending on the type of the Treasury (middle-office or front-office, see Part 2 of the book), ALM can also play a crucial role in offering funding sources. Structural maturity mismatch should be steered within settled structural liquidity limits, which description should be explicitly stated in the subsequent policies.
- Risk management and controls. Scope of assessment includes assessment of liquidity risk strategy and liquidity risk tolerance (and its interconnection with RAS), organizational framework (policies and procedures for risk identification, measurement, management, monitoring and reporting), liquidity contingency plans and stress testing. Based on such overall assessment of liquidity, regulators determine the need to apply specific liquidity measures – and quantify specific liquidity requirements for the bank (in addition to common requirements or their levels).

  As well as regarding capital management, ALM should ensure that the documents and answers provided to the regulator are in line with the given statements within other areas of assessment.

To conclude, ALM plays an important role in SREP, not visible on the first sight, but tremendously large if taken separately each of the questions of the supervisory inspections. ALM is the only expert in some of the topics, is the user in other areas, and is a mentor to the management board, ensuring that the bank functions within a holistic picture of risks and opportunities.

Chapter 14
Scope of ALM Involvement for Different Banks

Of course, ALM's activities in large and small banks, in head offices and in subsidiaries, in banks operating on well developed markets and in developing economies are quite different.

The differences are more noticeable when considering extreme cases, therefore, below two sub-chapters are devoted to banks, which differ according to their size of (and the share in) the market, and to banks operating in countries with different economic development. Difference of ALM activities in banks with different legal status (being the group entity or a subsidiary) was already covered in Chapter 12. All intermediary cases would have mixed characteristics, common for banks inside those groups where two or more criteria are fulfilled.

14.1 ALM Role for Banks with Different Market Shares

As it was mentioned in Chapter 13 ALM role and scope of activities is very much dependent on regulatory view (how supervisory authorities categorize and treat the bank) and internal structure of the bank itself.

Any regulatory authority (the National central bank/the National resolution authority or any authority responsible for local financial markets operations) has an aim to ensure stability of the economy and to defend participants and customers of financial markets from unexpected negative developments. With regard to banks, regulators rightfully consider banks with large market shares potentially harmful for the economy and customers (this was proved in the crisis in 2007 and triggered new development of additional regulatory controls and constraints for the large banks). If a large bank fails, it will trigger a domino-effect, if a lot of other financial institutions and companies have interconnections with the failed one. If many (or even majority) of banks in some economy fail – there won't be enough reserved funds to return money back to customers (as deposits may be requested immediately, but loans will continue to be held till initial maturity). Not always governments have (or want to use) government funds to nationalize failed banks and maintain stability of the economy. That is why after the 2007 crisis European regulators developed a three step supervisory framework for preventing harmful failures of banks.

Box 14.1. Recovery and Resolution Planning

The crisis of 2007 showed in many jurisdictions that the principle "too big to fail" does not work. Even big banks may fail under certain circumstances. As no one knows if some of the events are to occur in the future again or not – for economies it would be safer if there is a mechanism preventing

https://doi.org/10.1515/9783110669763-019

failure of such institutions elaborated. Constantly updated package of regulatory rules and principles aimed to address this question as well. By 2020 it was already clear that phases, which a bank may undergo under all possible spectra of circumstances, can be represented by the following list:
- Going concern
- Bank-driven recovery
- Authority-driven recovery and/or resolution
- Resolution involving external funds

Under *going concern* a bank should execute the ICAAP procedures, fulfill minimum regulatory requirements for own funds and liquidity ratios. Banks should indicate in the risk appetite framework the levels, reaching which will trigger *a recovery situation* for a bank (a situation, when a bank constitutes that its development does not go in line with the approved strategy and additional measures helping to return to a sustainable going-concern situation should be enforced). These levels (recovery triggers) and measures (recovery options), as well as description of step-by-step process of escalation (including informing the supervisors) and execution of the recovery options, together constitute a recovery plan. Each bank is responsible for drafting a recovery plan, outlining recovery options, not applying any state support measures.

When all recovery options were implemented, nothing more left unused, but the situation of the bank still did not return to the normal business, authorities may decide that the bank should be resolved. For such purposes authorities have to draft *a resolution plan*, usually with a help of the bank. The resolution authority defines the appropriate resolution strategy for the bank, while the bank itself is responsible for preparation of the resolution measures implementation. The final execution decision will be made by the authorities. Execution of the resolution plan should not be planned with any state support, but on a case-by-case basis it might be used.[1]

When regulators decide on the resolution strategy, there can be two options to consider: (a) normal liquidation (ordinary insolvency regime) and (b) resolution (according to BRRD[2] regime). The normal liquidation means that all banking operations are stopped; bank's wind-down is executed according to the national legal liquidation framework; shareholders/stakeholders and customers are paid their own bankruptcy distribution rate; interactions with the market/other entities of the same banking group are not specifically taken into account.

Under resolution, on the contrary to normal liquidation, the bank's operations continue according to the resolution plan; bank resolution is executed according to BRRD in combination with national liquidation framework; shareholders/stakeholders/customers should (in the end) be in a better situation than in the bankruptcy case; specifics of the banking group and its interactions with the market/other entities are taken into account. Regulators may decide in favor of resolution, when by failure of this bank maintenance of critical functions for economy is endangered, or financial stability of the market is endangered.

BRRD foresees potential implementation of four different resolution tools for resolution process:
- Sale-of business tool:[3] sale of parts of the balance sheet to an investor, liquidation of the rest of the institution.
- Bridge-institution tool:[4] transfer of parts of the balance sheet to a new legal entity, liquidation of the rest of the institution.

---

1 For example, by means of European Deposit Insurance System, according to Deposit Guarantee Scheme directive 2014/49/ EU.

2 Bank recovery and resolution directive 2014/59/EU.

3 Art. 38/39 BRRD II.

4 Art. 40/41 BRRD II.

- Asset separation tool:[5] transfer of assets and liabilities to an asset management vehicle ("bad bank"), continuation of the more focused/concentrated rest of the institution (core business and the critical functions).
- Bail-in tool:[6] off-setting of losses/conversion of eligible liabilities into equity (loss absorption and recapitalization), continuation of the institution. This instrument can be used in combination with other instruments.

Supervisory authorities require that the institution must support the resolution strategy by ensuring resolvability in several areas.[7] First, banks need to ensure that there are sufficient MREL instruments available to cover loss absorption and recapitalization needs in a resolution scenario. Second, working instructions of how loss absorption and subsequent conversion of MREL instruments into equity would be conducted (the bail-in playbook) should be elaborated. Moreover, financial and operational continuity and work in other areas (legal, governance, IT) should be ensured.

Regulators divide banks into groups (globally significant, other significant, other under direct supervision and the rest ones) in order to defend their economies. The larger and more significant the institution, the more attention the regulators will address to it. This attention is reflected in more frequent and intense supervision (including SREP) and reporting requests, in additional quantitative requirements to own funds and liquidity ratios (e.g., SyRB, P2R and P2G, individual add-ons), resolution according to BRRD as preferred resolution strategy regarding severe adverse circumstances. The simplest and the smallest institutions, for which no critical functions or interconnections in the economy can be identified, stay within a standard reporting schedule and list of reports, with Basel III capital and liquidity requirements (the Pillar I requirements) and go under normal liquidation in case of default.

Large market share of the bank makes banks look and act differently not only from the regulatory point of view (that is somehow consequence of the bank's size). The reason that made the banks act differently is, of course, the scope of the products and the depth of penetration to the economy. The nature of a large bank is that it has a great amount of deals, which it must settle and account; the products possess diverse options, which need to be correctly priced. Being strictly observed by regulators, large banks have no place for ambiguity between the functions and working lines. Having much to lose (large profits upstreaming to the shareholders and large bonuses allowed to the managers), large banks try to defend themselves by implementing up-to-date IT solutions and inviting best-of-the-market employees and consulting agencies. With regards to IT solutions, investments are a usual line of budget for such companies. Although for large banks automation is often harder due to possible mergers and acquisitions (M&A) of the past and necessity to integrate different databases into the same core banking system.

5 Art. 42 BRRD II.

6 Art. 43/44 BRRD II.

7 Seven dimensions of resolvability are defined in the "SRB Expectations for banks 2020."

At the same time, smaller banks are only specializing on specific products and/ or target specific group of clients. They have a smaller scale of business, amount of deals is comparably low, as well as profits. Frequently these banks are fighting for many years for having the "black zero" – insignificant amount of positive financial result, while rounding in large scale volumes equal to zero. Of course, such banks rarely have a budget for investments either in IT development, or in employees/ their education or consulting. In such banks situations often appear, when lack of staff prevents from proper split of responsibilities and some ambiguity in split of functions can take place.

It can be concluded (see summary in Table 14.1), due to the nature of the bank and regulatory attention to the institution, ALM in a larger bank should be aware of much more regulatory requirements, about specifics of accounting in capital or liquidity planning of different products and options. ALM in a large bank should be able to elaborate more measures for recovery and resolution and should defend the bank in each regulatory inspection. Dependent on resolution strategy and/or on

Table 14.1: Differences of ALM in small and large banks.

	Large market share	**Small market share**
Regulatory view		
– intensity of supervision	– more frequent and intense supervision and reporting	– standard reporting
– capital and liquidity requirements	– additional quantitative capital and liquidity requirements (buffers)	– standard Pillar I capital and liquidity requirements
– resolution strategy	– resolution under BRRD	– liquidation under normal insolvency
Internal banks' view		
– nature of the bank	– large volumes of deals – variety and optionality of products – deep penetration to the economy – large profits (and large bonuses)	– comparably low amount of deals – specialization on some product types – targeting some specific client group – fighting for profit (at least the "black zero")
– IT needs and problems	– budget is allocated to up-to-date IT solutions – difficulties of integration of IT systems after M&As	– no budget for investments in IT – volume of deals enables almost manual calculations

Table 14.1 (continued)

	Large market share	Small market share
– staff characteristic	– budget is allocated to best professionals/education of staff and consulting	– no budget for education and consulting, one person responsible for many fields
– conflicts of interest	– prudentially restricted and monitored	– ambiguity in split of functions is not excluded
ALM view		
– ALM risk management	– more knowledge on regulatory framework and product characteristics is required	– learning from the market is possible, time for implementation is prolonged
– BS structure targeting	– M&A activities require quantification of impact on capital and liquidity	– wider angle on the balance sheet and available methods enables to construct a holistic picture
– Price benchmarking	– statistical methods are appropriate – IT tools enable correct pricing of optionality of products	– internally constructed models should be based on grounded assumptions
– Resources allocation	– more possibilities for resource allocation optimization	– calculations can be done manually deal by deal and ensure high transparency

business plans of the bank ALM in a larger bank might be needed to become a part of M&A activities, elaborating and checking the impacts of different resolution/disentanglement options on capital and liquidity ratios. Large amount of deals makes statistical methods appropriate and implemented modern IT tools make their execution available. This enables correct accounting and pricing of a large variety of products. When there are many diverse operations, there are more ways for optimization of resource allocation.

Although ALM work in a larger bank seems to be more exciting, ALM experience in a smaller bank also has its advantages. First, ALM does not lose any of its initial functions and must defend the bank's balance sheet from negative developments. With a smaller and simpler balance sheet, checking the impacts and suggesting measures may be easier. Second, supervisors will not require assessment or implementation of the recent regulatory developments already in a consultation stage. That means that the bank has time to observe and learn how some requirements are executed by larger players in the market. As no budget was provided to sophisticated models elaboration and IT solutions, many ALM tasks are executed manually, which (a) increases transparency of results and (b) increases practical knowledge of ALM managers. At the same time, for a small bank it is more difficult to get benchmarking, and internally constructed models should be based on grounded assumptions, which even further improve the ability to see from a wide angle and to construct a holistic picture by the ALM manager.

14.2 ALM Role For Banks Operating in Different Market Environments

ALM managers of equal knowledge and experience can't execute their work in the same way in banks operating on a developed market and in banks from emerging markets. Although best practice is shared worldwide, it is not possible (and sometimes not needed) to be implemented everywhere. In order to understand what defines peculiarities of an ALM role in developed and developing financial markets, one should compare economic and regulatory environments.

Developed markets represent the best available practice in terms of availability of instruments and products (including products with embedded options, various derivatives). Usually these markets are liquid, each deal can be easily executed at each moment of time, and maturities of instruments are almost not limited. The other side of liquidity is that overall developed economies have more money available for investing, causing for banks a problem of excess liquidity, which should be effectively managed. This is hindered by usually a low rate environment, as developed economies maintain stable low levels of inflation, and operate hard currencies with low volatilities. Overall higher level of satisfaction makes customers in such environments more reliable on governments and banks, they keep life-long relations within one bank, and their behavior is not impulse-based and can be modeled.

Emerging markets often show only one-sided, not balanced development. This causes such problems on the markets as lack of some types of instruments (e.g., derivatives). Weaker currencies, higher inflation, and dependency on only one economic stream of income makes these countries exposed to high volatility of interest rates and prices, illiquid or even non-existent long-term debt and hedging instruments. As a consequence of economic development, the majority of people lack financial knowledge and perceive banks as non-reliable organizations. It is reflected in anxious behavior of customers, who are making sudden decisions, often based on interpretation of news and not analysis of facts.

Banking supervisory environment also differs for developed and developing markets. Main characteristic and aim of regulators on developed markets is to implement common principles in all the countries and to exclude possibilities of any kind of arbitrage. Accounting standards and risk management practices are unified and standardized. Therefore, developed economies are represented by almost full coverage of legislative topics, the principles are detailed and explicitly defined, and all discrepancies are restricted. Any possible conflicts of interest are also prudentially restricted and monitored.

Emerging markets often try to copy best practice even in supervisory areas, although they always need time to adjust their financial systems and, thus, are often postponed in implementation. Meanwhile their local standards are in place, which are sometimes stricter, sometimes do not cover all aspects considered in best practice legislation. Mentioned earlier, differences of market environments make local supervising authorities restrict some operations or products, or, on the contrary, be more loyal to some types of risk.[8] As an expected consequence, internal conflicts of interest in organizations can also not be fully covered by the legislation, and some ambiguity in split of functions is not excluded.

Described in Table 14.2, market and regulatory peculiarities on different markets define the role and scope of responsibilities of ALM in a bank. Developed markets raise more challenges for ALM in part of greater variety of products in the balance sheet and risks to be managed. At the same time – there are also available instruments for risk management (in particular for hedging). The models and approaches are defined by supervisory authorities, which results on one hand in their less customization and on the other hand require from ALM only understanding of these models, their invention is not needed.

Table 14.2: Differences of ALM in banks operating on developed and developing markets.

	Developed markets	Undeveloped markets
Market environment		
– products and instruments	– high availability and variety of instruments and products	– lack of some instruments/ products – low liquidity of the market – short maturities
– risk/return characteristics	– excess liquidity, low/ negative rates	– high inflation => higher and very high interest rates – high volatility of rates/prices
– customers' behavior	– customers have life-long relations with banks	– lack of financial knowledge – high anxiety of society, low level of trust to banks/government

8 There were many such cases observed worldwide, such examples are: regulatory caps on client rates for loans in period of high inflation in Belarus; or insufficient concern of the Czech supervisor about “cliff effect” of liabilities outflow during next days after LCR consideration in period of excess liquidity in the market.

Table 14.2 (continued)

	Developed markets	Undeveloped markets
Regulatory environment		
– legislative coverage of topics	– most principles are explicitly defined – discrepancies are restricted	– not always recommendations are defined – usually several years in delay from market best practice implementation
– standardability of accounting/risk requirements	– unified accounting and regulatory principles and risk management practices	– local approaches differ from unified accounting and regulatory principles (like Basel, etc.) – unjustified restrictions on some products
– conflicts of interest	– prudentially restricted and monitored	– ambiguity in split of functions is not excluded
ALM implications		
– ALM risk management	– high hedging possibilities – transformation result management	– limited hedging possibilities
– BS structure targeting	– low margin consideration – liquidity buffer management – asset sensitive balance sheet composition management	– high market volatility consideration – liability sensitive balance sheet composition management
– Price benchmarking	– need for embedded options pricing – high possibilities to construct internal curve – special attention on retail saving accounts pricing targeting	– simpler approaches can be applied – limited possibilities to construct internal curve
– Resources allocation	– multi-dimensional resource allocation optimization (many criteria available)	– very straightforward principles for resource allocation can be applied

As for the “guardian of the balance sheet” developed markets set for ALM a task to manage an asset sensitive balance sheet in low margins environment. For such a balance sheet floating rate loans and sticky retail deposits are a usual characteristic. Therefore, ALM has to pay precise attention to liquidity buffer management, maturity transformation targeting and saving accounts repricing. To stimulate or de-stimulate some business-line, different profitability/resource consumption metrics are at disposal for ALM.

On the contrary to the developed markets, emerging economies do not provide deep and liquid market of available risk management instruments. A bit to compensate it, it is worth mentioning, that there is also rather low diversity of products that banks provide. The risk comes mainly from the economic shocks, which regulators try to regulate with available recourses (not always corresponding to the best practices). As a result, supervisory authorities do not request highly sophisticated models covering all risk aspects to be in place, what makes ALM responsibilities execution rather simpler, applying often very straightforward principles addressing the main risk, which endanger banks' sustainability on a short-term horizon.

Balance-sheet in emerging financial markets is usually liability sensitive, meaning no swaps available, assets being very sticky, retail deposits more volatile with lower core stable amount. Liquidity buffer constitutes lower part of the balance sheet than the one in developed markets and requires fewer incentives for its profitable placement. Only fulfillment of all settled limits should be thoroughly controlled. Moreover, ALM needs to deal constantly with high market volatility that makes ALM operation closer to its role and tasks in a crisis environment.

Chapter 15
ALM Role in Crisis

According to conclusions in Part 1, crises repeat in a cycle of ~10 years. So as the book is being written probably during the most severe crisis in the 21st century, an immediate outbreak of the next one is not very likely. Nevertheless, ALM always should have in place methods and principles of managing the bank even in a crisis.

ALM participation in banks' processes in crisis intensifies many times. It embraces all areas of ALM: liquidity and funding; capital adequacy; IRRBB and the FTP. In general, for each area there's a predefined plan of actions that should be applied if there is an increase of severity of the crisis.

First, *liquidity* should be maintained on a sufficient level. A bank can survive a year without profit but will not survive even a day without liquidity. The following stacking order of actions should be applied, depending on how deep a bank gets into a liquidity trouble.

1) Corporate/retail deposits repricing (down) should be initiated, in order to maintain liquidity on the sufficient stable level.

   It is important to consider behavior of clients, how stable their relations with a particular bank are, and actions of the peers in the market – in order not to send wrong signals. For example, significant increase of interest rates on deposits can not only harm the net interest result, but also fail to achieve the aim of maintaining liquidity – the customers may consider this as an SOS-signal of a bank balancing on the edge of survival. Although, in some markets with strong supporting mechanisms from the state (deposit guarantee schemes) retail customers will feel safe investing their money (up to a certain amount) even in a weaker bank, knowing that in the worst case they would only have to wait until some other bank takes over the claims on their deposits.

2) Negotiations with other financial institutions on prolongation/new placements of middle- and long-term funding should be started. As crisis may imply also closing/decreasing counterparty limits, this action should be executed rather early – before decisions of other institutions are made.

   Here under other financial institutions the central banks facilities are also meant. The central banks, trying to support the economy, usually provide

https://doi.org/10.1515/9783110669763-020

additional funding facilities (e.g., Targeted longer-term refinancing operations (TLTRO) from ECB,[1] or other types of collateralized funding[2]).
3) For banks having the mother company (see Chapter 12), a short- or middle-term liquidity support from the head office should be prealigned.
4) For extremely urgent cases loan transfers to the head office or other financial institutions should be prepared. With regard to types of transfers, their several options can be in place: either a "true-sale" – complete reloading of the client from one financial institution to another (in this case, clients' consent should be obtained, what increases the timing of this measure), or a silent funded risk participation, when another institution just provides a cash collateral for the loan (the word "silent" here means that the client may not be informed about this deal).
5) As a very ultimate measure, initiation of asset repayment by clients should be executed. This measure, more than the other, impacts the bank's reputation and hinders its further recovery.

Second, there should be in place more intense monitoring of *capital* position (current and future) and the impacts of the crisis development. For that more frequent and up to date capital forecasts should be elaborated, quantitative assessment of capital measures should be prepared (RWA optimization/transfer, additional capital measures in different forms of capital), time for execution should be also considered.

For a case of crisis, the capital action plan should contain the following steps:
1) Quantification of the potential capital hit from different factors, such as:
   a. FX rate change
      i. Depreciation of domestic currency against strong currencies will mean that portion of strong currency denominated loans (and, thus, RWA) will increase – having negative impact on capital adequacy.
      ii. In the case of large investments (participations in other entities) made in weaker currencies, their depreciation will cause negative change of currency translation reserve as a part of other comprehensive income and decrease of capital and capital adequacy, simultaneously.

1 A first series of TLTROs was announced in 2014, a second series (TLTRO II) in 2016 and a third series (TLTRO III) in 2019 (available until 2021). TLTROs were offering banks long-term funding at attractive conditions, usually linked to under specific criteria eligible loans granted by banks to corporate clients and households.

2 For example, Czech National Bank announced in 2020 a program, according to which funding in a form of REPO transactions for three months will be provided to banks under collateral of mortgage bonds issued by the banks (https://www.cnb.cz/en/financial-markets/money-market/parameters-of-the-liquidity-providing-repo-operations/eligibility-criteria-for-mortgage-bonds-and-haircut-settings/).

iii. For head offices of banking groups, the influence will be three-fold – first, depreciation of local currencies of subsidiaries will decrease consolidated in a stronger currency RWA (with a positive effect on capital adequacy), second, already mentioned currency translation reserve change, third, local currencies depreciation will decrease consolidated loss (and it will have an immediate positive impact on capital adequacy) and profit (what will have a delayed negative impact on capital – until the audit of financial result, after which profit is allowed to be recognized in own funds).

b. Moratorium on lending and/or repayments
   i. For example, during the 2020 crisis regulators reacted fast and released guidelines on moratoria on loan repayments to support both customers and banks. For banks that meant that expected returns of liquidity, decreases of RWA and planned interest income (depending on the state, moratoria included a ban on both – interest payments and the notional amount of a loan) would not happen – having their subsequent impacts on capital adequacy. At the same time, though, the moratorium on repayments helped banks not to account past-due loans (and definitely in crisis there would have been such) as NPL, and not to reflect lowering of loan portfolio quality and decrease of capital adequacy.
   ii. When a government moratorium on loans repayments comes in place, a natural reaction of banks would be to stop/to slow down new lending, which would again have impact on future RWA and financial result.

c. Provisioning (loan loss provisions)
   i. Crisis usually means (although it was not observed in 2020) an extremely fast increase of forbearance and booking additional provisions/losses against capital.
   ii. In 2020 regulators made exceptions for banks in form, that they didn't have to account automatic forbearance due to acceptance of moratoria or public guarantees. That meant provisions could be postponed to the next year (or next years) when banks would be returning to going concern patterns.

d. Other impacts, including bond portfolio revaluation (and impacting capital through OCI), expected additional taxes/other losses, etc.

2) Estimation of the capital levels after the impacts and comparison to the regulatory requirements. In the crisis of 2020, regulators applied already predefined scenarios of capital reliefs: starting from immediate reaction of the ECB allowing temporarily using P2G and CCB for covering the losses resulting from the crisis, and followed by other supervising authorities decreasing local CCyB ratios until the moment when economies show they are on a recovery path.

3) Preparation of actions to counterbalance the potential capital shortfall:
   a. RWA optimization
      RWA optimization can come from (a) an enhancement of IT systems, correcting mistakes, increasing granularity, and reflection of more details of deals allowing (b) application of specific regulations for specific types of loans resulting in risk weights decrease. As an example, the moving from a standardized approach to an internal ratings-based approach, at least for some types of assets, can serve. Other examples are coming in the Basel IV regulations (see Chapter 16).

      At this stage the available to be "optimized" RWA should be estimated and/or the phase of ongoing activities should be stated.
   b. RWA transfer
      As in the case of loan transfers for liquidity purposes, RWA transfers to the head office or other financial institutions can be done. In addition to the true-sale and silent funded risk participation options, an unfunded risk participation can be applied in some cases. This method is based on providing by some financial organization a guarantee that in the case of customer's default it would cover the losses for the bank, which has granted the loan. Of course, the guarantee should be of the same amount and tenor, as the loan. It is important to consider that the guarantor should have a significantly better risk weight than the loan (due to a better rating, country or type of the guarantor), so that the operation pays off.

      For this option target volume and exact deals should be prepared, current status of the implementation should be stated.
   c. Other local measures with quantification of the impacts (which can include CAPEX reduction, increasing of profitability, etc.) should be assessed and (when possible and feasible) executed.
   d. As a last resort, applications for capital injections of different forms should be prepared.
      i. T2 subordinated loans can be injected or subordinated bonds can be issued up to their maximum amount of regulatory requirements for T1 and total capital difference in capital terms.
      ii. Additional T1 capital in the form of a perpetual loan or a bond can be injected/issued up to the maximum amount of regulatory requirements for CET1 and T1 difference in capital terms.
      iii. CET1 share capital issuance.

      For these actions the timing should be taken into account: most of these actions require regulatory approval (any injections of CET1 should be approved by the supervisory authority,[3] any conversions of lower type of capital into

3 Article 28 CRR.

better quality capital should be approved by the supervisory authority, as they imply redemption of own funds instruments[4]).
4) Estimation of capital surplus/shortfall after all actions.

Third, from the banking book management perspective, the right incentives should be given to business lines outlining and supporting decisions made in other ALM areas. In particular, to stimulate deposits collection and de-stimulate lending, *FTP curves* must be revaluated accordingly and/or a steering margin can be applied. It is important to take into account maturity transformation result (in particular, coming from maturities mismatch of assets and liabilities) – and through the adjustment of steepness of the FTP curve manage the scale of possible negative impacts on the net interest result.

Fourth, the recovery measures should be constantly reassessed, whether some of them were already applied by the bank in the process of liquidity, capital, or financial result maintenance. The bank should keep track of its capacity to execute the recovery plan and inform the regulators accordingly if some of the resources are going to be used up.

4 Articles 77–78 CRR.

Chapter 16
After-Crisis ALM

The evidence of important future trends in banking was clear before the crisis 2020. Some of these trends were captured in regulatory framework and were ready to be implemented in practice. By the beginning of the 2020s it was expected that the era of regulatory uncertainty would come finally to its end[1] with completion of the reform process. The crisis of 2020 itself demonstrated that regulators are now much better prepared having the mechanisms to support economies, than it was before. Although new circumstances revealed some missing details, pointing out that there are still many unsolved questions and that the regulatory development will hardly ever stop.

The vital trends that will impact not only banking overall, but the ALM as well, can be split into the following groups:
- Business planning with accounting of the *economic perspective*
- Regulatory reporting according to *proportionality* and *cherry-picking* principles
- Understanding that *crises are driven not only by economic/financial factors*
- *MREL*[2] *targeting* and harmonization of resolution approaches across jurisdictions
- Increased numbers and regularity of *M&A*
- Even further continued *digitalization*
- *Globalization*

16.1 ALM Role within the Economic Perspective

Traditionally banks aimed under any circumstances to comply with regulatory ratios imposed on capital adequacy, liquidity level, and balance sheet structure – categories in ALM scope of responsibility. In November 2018 ECB issued guidance,[3] where named this approach the normative perspective, outlining also its necessary interconnection to the opposed to it economic perspective. From then on, the normative (regulatory) perspective officially was not considered sufficient on its own anymore, and prudent asset and liability management always appeared to be informed by the economic perspective. While elaborating credible management actions, ALM should take into

1 Work on Basel III began back in 2009, its final part was agreed on only in December 2017, and the full transition phase lasts until 2027. By the crisis of 2020 regulators will have already passed 11 out of 18 years of the regulatory reform.

2 Minimum requirement for own funds and eligible liabilities aim to ensure that sufficient funds are readily available to absorb potential losses and recapitalize the bank in the event of resolution.

3 ECB Guide to the internal liquidity adequacy assessment process (ILAAP) and ECB Guide to the internal capital adequacy assessment process (ICAAP), November 2018.

https://doi.org/10.1515/9783110669763-021

account results of assessment according to the economic perspective as well: in particular, outflows of liquidity and/or losses impacting capital in hypothetical worst-case scenarios, which were not captured in the normative perspective.

The same idea was introduced earlier in IFRS 9 standard (effective for annual periods beginning on or after 1 January 2018)[4] with regard to loan loss provisions, when losses, which actually didn't yet occur, should be accounted in financial result and impact the capital position. Introduced in IFRS 9 standard recognition of financial assets impairment in 3 stages implied that in the 1st stage (as soon as a financial instrument was originated or purchased) 12-month expected credit losses should already be recognized in profit or loss. In the 2nd stage if the credit risk increases significantly and is not considered low, full lifetime expected credit losses should be recognized in profit or loss. Finally, in the 3rd stage if the credit risk of a financial asset increases to the point that it is considered credit-impaired, banks' P&L is even more impacted as the interest income from the loan is calculated based on its amortized cost (its initial amount less provisions).

Economic nature of financial categories is also a part of IRRBB (see Box 11.2), which takes into account not only the short-term effects on profitability, but also the economic value of the institution's equity on the whole horizon of its existence.

As a result of economic perspective introduction and implementation in different banking areas, the bank will have to keep larger liquidity and capital surpluses in the long run. It is argued by bankers that this requirement diminishes the net interest margin, already rather low on developed markets. Nevertheless, there were studies already conducted,[5] proving the evidence that banks with higher capital ratios have a better risk/revenue trade-off, meaning that they generate the same level of profit at lower risk. Supervisory authorities outline[6] that those banks that have strong balance sheets are more capable of supporting their customers through the cycle. At the same time – in order to have a positive financial result they have to refocus their business models, having better control over costs and investments. ALM can be helpful here in both aspects: stabilizing the balance sheet and giving proper targets for development of new business model.

16.2 ALM in Times of Regulatory Requirements Differentiation

Earlier in the book it was described that regulatory attention to smaller and larger banks differs significantly: starting from different reporting requests (600 data points

4 IFRS 9 Financial Instruments, IFRS Standards.

5 F. Mergaerts R.V. Vennet, "Business Models and Bank Performance: A Long-Term Perspective," *Journal of Financial Stability 22*, 2016, 57–75.

6 P. Hakkarainen, *The EU Regulatory Environment – Room for Improvement*, speech at the Governance, Risk Management and Compliance conference, Frankfurt am Main, 19 November 2019.

for small banks as opposed to almost 40,000 for large banking groups a year[7]) and finishing with different quantitative requirements on capital and liquidity. This differentiation becomes even more targeted, as regulatory authorities point out that some types of exposures are more threatening to local economies, whereas others can be, on the contrary, stimulated.

One of the examples is the systemic risk buffer, introduced on a subset of exposures.[8] Competent authorities will be able to choose a specific type of exposure (inside categories of retail/legal entities, collateralized/non-collateralized exposures) and assign to keep higher capital surplus (buffer) for it. Another example is the Basel initiative of sectoral counter-cyclical buffer.[9] By initiation of this buffer macro-prudential authorities try to enhance banks' resilience of the materialization of sector-specific risks. ALM will have to enhance capital planning with additional steps, which are similar to currently elaborated counter-cyclical capital buffer calculation.

Box 16.1. Capital Planning When Requirements Are Applied to Specific Types of Exposures

Usually capital planning for each moment of time implies several steps. They are as follows:

1) Definition of own funds absolute amount
2) Definition of risk weighted assets (RWA)
3) Calculations of capital adequacy ratio (CAR, as a relation of own funds to RWA)
4) Opposing of the calculated CAR to the regulatory (or internal) requirement and determination of available surplus

In cases when to some types/subsets of exposures a specific requirement with regard to capital is applied, the calculation is enhanced with additional steps. Currently CRD IV prescribes for all banks to calculate CCyB, if a bank has granted a loan to a borrower, which country of registration has imposed such buffers. To clearly describe the principle of calculations, a simplified example is given below.

The capital planning is made for a hypothetical banking group, which operates in Germany (CCyB = 0%, Basel Pillar 1 requirement 8% and capital conservation buffer 2,5% applied) and has subsidiaries in Luxemburg (CCyB = 0.25% and will increase to 0.5%) and Hong Kong (CCyB = 1%), see Table 16.1.

---

7 A. Enria, *Regulation, Proportionality and the Sustainability of Banking*, speech at the Retail Banking Conference "Creating Sustainable Financial Structures by Putting Citizens First" of European Savings Bank Group, Brussels, 21 November 2019.

8 Final guidelines on the appropriate subsets of sectoral exposures to which competent or designated authorities may apply a systemic risk buffer in accordance with Article 133(5)(f) of Directive 2013/36/EU, EBA/GL/2020/13, EBA, 30 September 2020.

9 ECBS Guiding principles for the operationalization of a sectoral countercyclical capital buffer, BCBS 28 November 2019. These principles have not been included as part of the Basel Standards and are relevant for jurisdictions that voluntarily choose to implement a SCCyB at a national level. Currently Switzerland is the only jurisdiction where a SCCyB is already in place, while the Spanish government has introduced the legal basis for a SCCyB in Spain.

Table 16.1: Calculation of CCyB requirement for a banking group.

	Year 1	Year 2	Year 3	Year 4	
Own funds (A)	460	465	470	475	Step 1
RWA total (B), out of which	3200	3450	3550	3650	Step 2
RWA Hong Kong (B.1)	*850*	*890*	*930*	*980*	
RWA Luxemburg (B.2)	*300*	*330*	*350*	*380*	
Capital adequacy ratio (C) = (A)/(B)	14.38%	13.48%	13.24%	13.01%	Step 3
Capital requirement (D) = 8% + 2,5% + (E), out of which	10.79%	10.78%	10.81%	10.82%	Step 4b
Countercyclical capital buffer, group (E) = (B.1*E.1 + B.2*E.2)/(B)	0.29%	0.28%	0.31%	0.32%	Step 4a
Countercyclical capital buffer, Hong Kong (E.1)	*1.00%*	*1.00%*	*1.00%*	*1.00%*	
Countercyclical capital buffer, Luxemburg (E.2)	*0.25%*	*0.25%*	*0.50%*	*0.50%*	
Capital surplus (F) = (C – D) * (B)	**115**	**93**	**86**	**80**	Step 4

Steps 1–3 are executed without changes. Before Step 4 additional steps should be executed. During Step 4a (in the table) a weighted average CCyB for the banking group is calculated: (RWA Hong Kong * CCyB Hong Kong + RWA Luxemburg * CCyB Luxemburg)/RWA total. At Step 4b the calculated CCyB for the group is added to capital requirements: Pillar 1 requirement 8% + capital conservation buffer 2,5% + CCyB Group. Capital surplus now incorporates all expected regulatory requirements changes and can be used for business planning, resource allocation or further modelling.

When different systemic risk buffers are applied to different types of exposures, the calculation will be the same as in the example, and a weighted average SyRB for the bank will be calculated.

Another example is supporting factor[10] for small- and medium-sized enterprises (SME), a multiplier which decreases the risk weight of the exposure. It can only be applied if the maximum exposure amount owed by a client, for whom the SME supporting factor can be applied, is not higher than the regulatory predefined threshold.

One would relate internal ratings-based approaches for determining risk weights for exposures also to this category. Although, increased diversification of treatment of exposures does not mean that some banks by solving optimization task will be much more successful than the other. Regulatory authorities tried to avoid too much of internal optimization and set an output floor[11] – a lower limit for the

10 It was planned to be fully introduced by 28.06.2021 as part of CRR II and will range from 76.2% (for 2.5m € amounts) to 81.3% (for 6 m € amounts), depending on the amount of the exposure, but issued during the 2020 crisis CRR "quick-fix" (entered into force on 27.06.2020, before its initially planned date) already included this amendment.

11 A constraint on banks' overall leverage was also added in order to complement risk-based capital requirements. Under the revised standards, banks using internal models to calculate capital requirements must hold at least 72.5% of the capital, which would be held under the (typically more

risk-weighted assets that banks calculate with their internal models, giving them the freedom to use internal models while at the same time introducing a "safeguard." As many other regulatory updates, the output floor will have a gradual 5-year transitional phase-in, according to the BCBS, starting in 2022 (see Table 16.2) for institutions to adjust to the new requirement.[12]

Table 16.2: Output floor phase-in.

Output floor amount	**50%**	**55%**	**60%**	**65%**	**70%**	**72.5%**
Phase-in year	1 January 2022	1 January 2023	1 January 2024	1 January 2025	1 January 2026	1 January 2027

All in all, new approaches to proportionality and differentiation of requirements result in new challenges for banks and ALM in particular: (1) constantly changing environment gives need for multiple scenarios of balance sheet development; (2) scenario impacts are different across different commercial sectors, given their financial condition and creditworthiness; (3) targeting only specific types of borrowers may also impact liquidity plans; and (4) introduction of new capital buffers requirements, although with phase-in periods, brings huge uncertainty in long-term business planning.

Exactly in these times sustaining consistency across the institution and a stable and optimized balance sheet becomes critical for long-term steering of the bank. The same planning assumptions, signals, and benchmarking principles and the same inputs driving capital allocation and scenario assessment should be used for financial planning and strategic decisions. ALM here, as always, must execute the central function, which takes responsibility for assumptions and delivers a new set of management information to support the senior team, external communication, and supervisory dialogues.

16.3 ALM Preparing for Non-Financial Crises

The year 2020 showed that severe world crises are not always financially driven. A stable financial and banking system, well prepared to mitigate losses resulting from improper financial transactions can still be vulnerable to economic downturns due to any other factors (like pandemics, sanctions, wars, or climate change). Of course, one would argue that such force majeure events, usually categorized as low frequency high severity events, can be captured under operational risk calculations (in operational risk

conservative) standardized approach. This measure, which is designed to reduce unwarranted variability in banks' risk-weights, is known as the "output floor."

12 Policy Advice on the Basel III Reforms: Output Floor, EBA-Op-2019-09c, EBA, 2 August 2019.

RWA consuming capital surplus). Nevertheless, the consequences of such events may last for a rather long time, and banks should be prepared to overcome such periods in terms of sufficient capital and liquidity.

Banks will need to adopt their traditional asset and liability management approaches to understand how they are financially exposed to and affected by environmental risks. While speaking about wars, sanctions and pandemics – whole regions may face significantly unfavorable conditions, leading to breaks in supply chains, scarce demand, insufficient inflows, losses and past due loans, what would endanger banks in those regions or ones dealing with such counterparties. In the case of climate change, unusual heatwaves, droughts, storms, and other natural disasters will lead to economic and financial costs, which might also have an impact on banks' balance sheets.

With regard to climate change, supervisory authorities[13] outline also a second group of risk factors: transition risks. Given that economies will go from "brown" to "green," some sectors (and even countries) might suffer – those which are carbon-intensive, dependent on income from hydrocarbons export. And when banks are exposed to these sectors, they will be stressed as well.

ALM task will be to observe the holistic picture of the bank's business development and to have in advance prepared measures to mitigate adverse impacts on the balance sheet and capital. Exposures to countries, sectors, economies, which could be damaged by non-financial crisis, should be separately observed as components of capital forecasting and business planning, stress tests should incorporate scenarios, which would assess the scale of possible disasters connected with these types of exposures. To prevent breach of regulatory requirements, results of such stress test may be incorporated into internal capital and liquidity buffers, as well as accounted in recovery measures of the bank.

16.4 ALM Role in Resolution Strategy

As it was emphasized earlier, local regulatory (resolution) authorities decide on the strategy with regard to the resolution of a bank. As soon as the strategy is defined, banks obtain MREL target, compliance which would ensure that in the case of a failure, the bank will not damage the economy significantly.

MREL target will depend on the strategy, which regulator approves for the institution (for details see Box 14.1). If the competent authority has revealed neither any critical service, which the bank executes, nor financial stability endangerment, the institution can go under common liquidation, and no additional MREL requirements on top of the

13 A. Enria, *Regulation, Proportionality and the Sustainability of Banking*, speech at the Retail Banking Conference "Creating sustainable financial structures by putting citizens first" of European Savings Bank Group, Brussels, 21 November 2019.

own funds will be imposed. In this case ALM tasks seem to be untouched. However, legislators found out significant differences in liquidation processes across countries and are now considering aligning national insolvency triggers and adding a harmonized liquidation tool to the European banking toolbox[14] to avoid regulatory arbitrage or arguments on unequal treatment of banks across jurisdictions. This exercise would require ALM involvement in regulatory dialogues and additional reporting.

When a bank is considered significant enough to endanger financial stability, resolution authorities' assessment results in assigning to it a resolution strategy regarding its failure and additional MREL requirements are imposed on top of the own funds requirements. MREL target consists of loss absorbency amount (LAA, equal to capital requirements under stressed scenario, consisting of P1 + P2R), recapitalization amount (RCA, representing requirements for stressed conditions P1 + P2R, after the initial capital is fully consumed by the loss) and market confidence charge (MCC, equal to CBR less the amount maintained to meet the CCyB), according to updated in 2020 SRB logic.[15] In some rare and specific case, when a banking group is heterogeneous, SRB can decide on a specific add-on – adjustment for the inhomogeneity of the banking group. It may happen, when banks within a group operate under too much different regimes and execution of one resolution strategy (SPE – single point of entry, or MPE – multiple point of entry – resolution strategy) is not possible. MREL target relation to own funds requirements can be observed in Figure 16.1.

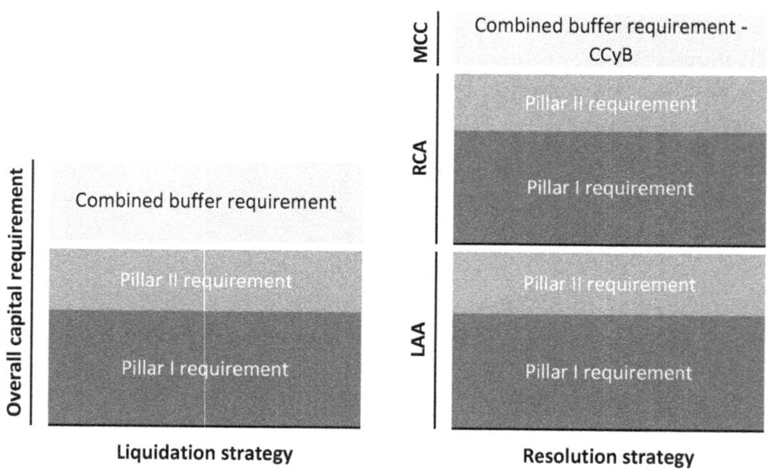

Figure 16.1: MREL target dependent on the resolution strategy.

14 K. Af Jochnick, *Challenges for the European Banking System*, speech at the ISDA conference on "EU Banking Reforms: Crossing the 't's' and dotting the 'i's' – Current & Future Priorities for Europe," 3 March 2020.

15 Minimum Requirement for Own Funds and Eligible Liabilities (MREL) SRB Policy under the Banking Package, SRB, 20.05.2020.

If the "resolution" add-ons are higher than the capital surplus of the bank, ALM is responsible to raise MREL eligible funding, and to maintain MREL amount on a sufficient level through the cycle. As far as by now there's no complete list of MREL eligible liabilities, each funding that fulfills the basic conditions[16] (including residual maturity in more than one year, not (retail) deposits covered by Deposit Guarantee Scheme, DGS, not liabilities against authorities or social insurance, not purchased by the institution itself), should be negotiated with the resolution authority if it can be considered as eligible. Although the legislative framework is constantly developing, and after clarity is reached, ALM task would be to optimize the funding/capital structure, in order to avoid unnecessary preloading of capital or excessive interest expenses.

16.5 ALM in Times of Digitalization and Globalization

Digitalization is always associated with new products, better services to the customers and promisingly increased profits of the bank. It has also an implication on the internal banking life in terms of simplifications of reporting and accumulating data for analysis.

Although competent authorities[17] have already pointed out that all innovations have the potential to create new risks, and digitalization and digital business models are not an exception. Digitalization might affect funding, with new digital tools allowing depositors to switch banks by means of a few clicks. That implies that deposits are becoming a less reliable source of funding, what should be accounted in ALM models and liquidity maintenance measures.

Some aspects of globalization counterbalance the threat that retail deposits are becoming less reliable due to digitalization (and for most commercial banks this is the core source of funding). With creation of a fully-fledged European deposit insurance scheme, it will act as a confidence mechanism for banking customers and will reduce the likelihood of bank runs.[18]

16.6 ALM Role in M&A

Any merger or acquisition is considered as a one-off unique extraordinary event. It is not included in the going concern scenario. When a banking group comes up with a decision to buy or sell an asset or entity (especially another bank) it triggers

16 Articles 44 (1) and 45(4) BRRD.

17 K. Af Jochnick, *Challenges for the European Banking System*, speech at the ISDA conference on "EU Banking Reforms: Crossing the 't's' and dotting the 'i's' – Current & Future Priorities for Europe," 3 March 2020.

18 P. Hakkarainen, The EU Regulatory Environment – Room for Improvement, speech at the Governance, Risk Management and Compliance conference, Frankfurt am Main, 19 November 2019.

changes in management on all levels, from accounting rules to human resources management. Of course, ALM will also take an active part in such activities. However, before describing the peculiarities of ALM, a few words are needed to justify why M&A are expected to happen more often in the current banking world.

Beginning in 2017 (and far before the crisis of 2020) more and more speeches of banking policy makers were outlining how the European banking sector is oversized. The chair of ECB's supervisory board, Andrea Enria, pointed out that although "the optimal size of the banking sector is hard to gauge, it seems clear . . . that the European banking sector is still too large."[19] Kerstin af Jochnick, member of the supervisory board of the ECB supports the idea of necessity of consolidation and outlines that market exits, as well as M&A are "beneficial for the European banking sector to . . . reap the benefits of economies of scale and improved risk-sharing."[20]

It was obvious for bankers and regulators,[21] that by continuing business as usual, banks are not able to show the same high profitability, as before (due to regulatory reforms and low interest rate environment). Moreover, in a crisis while the poor become even poorer and banks with smaller capital surplus are more prone to get into default, the rich can become even richer, and banks with larger initial capital surpluses can employ it with greater benefits in the long-run. Therefore, banks need to think wider, exploring opportunities of changing their businesses in a non-natural way. This idea is supported by a broad round of competent authorities' management, emphasizing that "weak profitability will remain a cause for concern for financial stability because it hampers banks' ability to build buffers against negative shocks. And it may also negatively affect banks' ability to support the real economy. Mergers have been put forward as one of the ways for banks to shore up profitability through cost efficiencies."[22]

19 A. Enria, *Is Less More? Profitability and Consolidation in the European Banking Sector*, presentation at the CIRSF Annual International Conference, Lisbon, 4 July 2019. It is worth mentioning that ECB vice presidents de Guindos and Constancio have expressed similar views. See L. De Guindos, *Euro Area Banks: The Profitability Challenge*, speech at the ABI annual conference "Banking Union and Basel III – Risk and Supervision 2019," Rome, 25 June 2019; and V. Constâncio, *Challenges Faced by the European Banking Sector*, speech at the Risk & Supervision Conference organized by Associazione Bancaria Italiana, Rome, 14 June 2017.

20 K. Af Jochnick, *Challenges for the European Banking System*, speech at the ISDA conference on "EU Banking Reforms: Crossing the 't's' and dotting the 'i's' – Current & Future Priorities for Europe," 3 March 2020.

21 "A number of structural indicators for the banking system that are regularly compiled by the ECB, such as market concentration shares, population per credit institution, population per branch, and assets per bank employee, support the view that there is room for consolidation in some markets and jurisdictions," according to Kerstin af Jochnick. See K. Af Jochnick, *Banking Performance, Competition and Financial Stability: A Supervisory View*, speech at the 7th Frankfurt Conference on Financial Market Policy "European Banking – Too Much Competition?" 15 November 2019.

22 K. Af Jochnick, *Banking Performance, Competition and Financial Stability: A Supervisory View*, speech at the 7th Frankfurt Conference on Financial Market Policy "European Banking – Too Much Competition?" 15 November 2019.

Until now M&A within banking groups across different countries were complicated by discrepancies in local legislations and bans on free capital and liquidity transfers over the borders. With regulators' plans[23] to unify first legislation for insolvency procedures, there's a tendency that cross-border M&A will also be unified sooner or later. For banks, and ALM functions as well, it is important to prepare for such projects, with the clear understanding of drivers of impacts on capital and liquidity and their timing.

Liquidity implications in the process of acquisition and/or disentanglement of assets usually happen the moment the price of the deal is paid or received. Let's consider two examples: regarding banks A and B, they are being consolidated (Figure 16.2), whereas in banks C and D, the latter is deconsolidated from the initial entity (Figure 16.3). For simplification, the price of the deal is assumed to be equal to NAV (net asset value of the acquired/disentangled entity).

Bank A			
Liquidity	150	900	Deposits
Loans	850		
		100	Equity
Total	**1000**	**1000**	

Bank B			
Liquidity	3	15	Deposits
Loans	17		
		5	Equity
Total	**20**	**20**	

Bank A + B			
Liquidity	148	915	Deposits
Loans	867		
Investment	5	105	Equity
Total	**1020**	**1020**	

Figure 16.2: Liquidity implications in case of consolidation of banks.

Bank C + D			
Liquidity	240	1190	Deposits
Loans	1050		
Investment	10	110	Equity
Total	**1300**	**1300**	

Bank D			
Liquidity	4	40	Deposits
Loans	50		
		10	Equity
Total	**54**	**50**	

Bank C			
Liquidity	246	1150	Deposits
Loans	1000		
		100	Equity
Total	**1246**	**1250**	

Figure 16.3: Liquidity implications in case of deconsolidation of banks.

As it can be seen from the basic examples of balance sheets, the liquidity position of the bank, which buys or sells an entity, is impacted by the price of the investment. The "liquidity" amount equals the sum (a difference) of liquidity positions of the two entities minus (plus) the amount paid (received) for the investment (disentanglement) at the date of closing the deal.

Among other liquidity considerations that appear regarding buying or selling a bank, are surpluses or shortfalls over the binding liquidity requirements. LCR or subsequent other liquidity requirement should be calculated for each new entity and when needed appropriate actions should be elaborated. It may turn out that some of the actions will impact the price of the deal, and the initial calculations will have to be repeated.

23 For example, 12th January 2021 ECB issued a Guide on the supervisory approach to consolidation in the banking sector.

In comparison to liquidity implications, impacts on capital are differentiated in terms of drivers and in terms of timing. Moreover, capital measures (when needed) require much more time for their implementation, than the ones to improve liquidity.

The timing issue appears, because there's always a time lag between signing of the contract and closing of the deal. This time lag usually lasts for several months and requires not only finishing all the requested documentation, to execute the needed preparatory procedures and assessments, but also getting approvals of the deal from the regulatory authority (or several in the case of a cross-border M&A deal).

At the moment of signing of the contract *for selling an entity* (or even before, when the intention to execute the deal is indicated, according to criteria for the sale to be highly probable) IFRS 5,[24] which regulates accounting of discontinued operations, comes in force. Shortly, IFRS 5 prescribes that assets must be measured as lower of their carrying amount and fair value less the costs to sell. That means that the financial result of the deal, when negative, should be immediately booked in financial statements and impact capital calculations.

This is shown in the tables in the example (see Figure 16.4): in case when the deal results in profit (so for the disentangled entity with NAV equal to 300 million in the example, the multiplier of the price to book value is more than 1), it has a delayed positive effect on the capital position of the initial bank (1.2–1)*300 = 60 million. In the left-hand table this is reflected at the moment of signing (but, of course, profit can be recognized in capital only after an external audit). The worst case for capital position is represented by no change in comparison to the one before the deal. As no losses occur, the intangible assets (10 million), which also represent one of the main drivers of capital changes, do not require any provisions or write-off and stay unchanged until the date of deal closing and disappear from the "mother" entity's balance sheet together with loans. For capital calculations that means simultaneous improvement of capital amount by amount of intangible assets of the sold entity and decrease of risk weighted assets by its RWA (1,500 million) less consolidation effect of intragroup RWA (which is the equity, assuming no more interbank deals existed). Also, at the moment of the final closing of the deal, the other comprehensive income in part of foreign currency translation reserve for revaluation of participations is reflected in the profit (in the example above this is positive and equals 30 million). Although it will not impact the capital position, as OCI was already part of capital, and will be transferred from the OCI component of the own funds to retained earnings, as the deal is closed and financial result due to FX rate fluctuations is fixed.

24 IFRS 5 Non-Current Assets Held for Sale and Discontinued Operations, IFRS Standards.

multiplier			1.2
	Before the deal	At signing	At closing
Own funds, *driven by changes in*	900	900	950
Intangible assets			-10
Profit and loss, *including*			90
Profit/loss on NAV			60
OCI			30
OCI			-30
RWA, *out of which*	6000	6000	4800
RWA of disentangled entity			1500
RWA intragroup			-300
Capital adequacy ratio	15.0%	15.0%	19.8%
Capital requirement	14.0%	14.0%	14.0%
Surplus/shortfall	**60**	**60**	**278**

multiplier			0.7
	Before the deal	At signing	At closing
Own funds, *driven by changes in*	900	820	820
Intangible assets		-10	
Profit and loss, *including*		-90	30
Profit/loss on NAV		-90	
OCI			30
OCI			-30
RWA, *out of which*	6000	6000	4800
RWA of disentangled entity			1500
RWA intragroup			-300
Capital adequacy ratio	15.0%	13.7%	17.1%
Capital requirement	14.0%	14.0%	14.0%
Surplus/shortfall	**60**	-20	**148**

Figure 16.4: Capital implications in case of selling a subsidiary bank.

The capital requirements in the tables in Figure 16.4 are taken as a possible value for representative purposes.

At the same time, regarding the selling below the NAV (in the example for NAV = 300 million and a multiplier equal to 0.7 of price to book value), the loss (0.7–1) * 300 million = –90 million is recognized in capital immediately in line with IFRS 5. If a bank did not have a solid capital position before the deal (it had insufficient surplus to cover the loss of the deal), it would result in a capital shortfall until the closing of the deal, when disentangled RWA counterbalance the capital effect. The impact on the capital is slightly counterbalanced by intangible assets of the sold entity, as they are written off (–10 million). The shortfall, of course, can be considered technical, as at the moment of closing of the transaction, the RWA of the sold entity won't be any more accounted on the balance sheet and in the capital calculations of the initial entity. Although for capital management and ALM overall, nevertheless, it means a task to elaborate for the temporary period capital measures that would allow the bank to fulfill obligatory requirements (for capital measures see Chapter 15, "ALM Role in Crisis").

If *buying an entity* the guiding IFRS standard will be IFRS 3.[25] The effects will be the opposite to the sale, whereas timing of the effects should be considered differently: according to IFRS 3, the acquisition date is the date on which the acquirer obtains control over another entity. It is generally the date on which the acquirer legally transfers the payment for the investment, acquires the assets and assumes the liabilities of another entity, in other words – it is the date of closing. All assets and liabilities are measured at acquisition date at fair value.

Not having the timing effect in place, for accounting and ALM it is important to understand if the bank acquires 100% of shares of another entity or only a portion. In the case of 100% of shares acquired, no non-controlling interest (NCI) appears, because the investor owns subsidiary's equity in full.

The example in Figure 16.5 again assumes an entity with NAV equal to 300 million, 1,500 million RWA, and 10 million intangible assets. It is assumed that 100% of shares are purchased.

If the price of the deal differs from the NAV of the acquired entity, goodwill appears. Goodwill is an asset that represents future economic benefits arising from the acquired asset. In a simplified example (without NCI), goodwill = price – NAV. For own funds calculation purpose, if goodwill is positive, it is recognized as an intangible asset and is deducted from own funds. An annual goodwill impairment test should be performed, but any impairment will be capital neutral, as impairment will trigger not only a decrease of goodwill (that is a deductible), but also losses, which would decrease the PL – another component of own funds. Sometimes, when capitalization of the investing bank was not solid enough, it may result that on a consolidated level in a capital shortfall (as in the left-hand table in Figure 16.5). This should be timely revealed by

25 IFRS 3 Business Combinations, IFRS Standards.

multiplier		1.1
	Before the deal	After the deal
Own funds, *driven by changes in*	900	860
Intangible assets (-)		10
Goodwill (-)		30
Price		330
NAV		300
RWA, *out of which*	6000	7200
RWA of acquired entity		1500
RWA intragroup		-300
Capital adequacy ratio	15.0%	11.9%
Capital requirement	14.0%	14.0%
Surplus / shortfall	**60**	**-148**

multiplier		0.6
	Before the deal	After the deal
Own funds, *driven by changes in*	900	1010
Intangible assets (-)		10
Gain on a bargain purchase (+)		120
Price		180
NAV		300
RWA, *out of which*	6000	7200
RWA of acquired entity		1500
RWA intragroup		-300
Capital adequacy ratio	15.0%	14.0%
Capital requirement	14.0%	14.0%
Surplus / shortfall	**60**	**2**

Figure 16.5: Capital implications in case of buying a bank.

ALM, indicated to the management board and appropriate mitigating measures should be elaborated and executed (when investment is still considered).

If goodwill is negative (so the entity is purchased below its NAV), then the difference between the price and the NAV is a gain on a bargain purchase. It is recognized in PL, as a gain on the acquisition and is included in the own funds after the audit of the profit.

Regarding M&A, ALM should take care of the possible change of the requirements after the purchase: according to the ECB Guide on the supervisory approach to consolidation in the banking sector mentioned earlier, the capital requirements in terms of P2R and P2G for a consolidated entity in general cases will be the weighted average of the P2R and P2G levels applicable to the two entities prior to the consolidation (exceptions are when entities are not under the SSM - then adaptations can be applied).

Other ALM concerns regarding an M&A deal are in the area of recovery and resolution, as the triggers might be breached during the deal, and resolution strategy may result in its amendments. This should be negotiated step by step with the competent authorities, jointly elaborating the appropriate plan for the new entity.

Conclusions

ALM is deeply involved in all banks' processes and plays a significant role in defining the future stance of the bank, notwithstanding its different spectrum of tasks in banks of different scale and background. ALM role, power, and responsibility increases even further in times of crisis and is crucial for banks' recovery after crises.

The contemporary trends in banking include economic perspective consideration, proportionality principles introduction, accounting for non-financial factors impacting business and leading to crises, new regulatory requirements and their harmonization across jurisdictions followed by higher frequency of M&A, continued further digitalization, and globalization. To achieve challenging goals, which are imposed by regulatory authorities in their struggles for a more stable and prosperous world financial system, and to support the shareholders in their wishes of higher RoE of the bank becomes the new ultimate task of ALM.

Selected Bibliography

2016 EU- Wide Stress Test Methodological Note. EBA, 24 February 2016.

Af Jochnick, K. *Banking Performance, Competition and Financial Stability: A Supervisory View*. Speech at the 7th Frankfurt Conference on Financial Market Policy "European Banking – Too Much Competition?" 15 November 2019.

Af Jochnick, K. *Challenges for the European Banking System*. Speech at the ISDA conference on "EU Banking Reforms: Crossing the 't's' and dotting the 'i's' – Current & Future Priorities for Europe," 3 March 2020.

Barlow, J. *The Pros and Cons of Centralizing Treasury*, June 2011, www.financeasia.com.

Barth, J.R., Caprio, G., Jr., and Levine, R. *Banking Regulation and Supervision: What Works Best?* National Bureau of Economic Research Working Paper, November 2002, No. 9323.

Basel III: A Global Regulatory Framework for More Resilient Banks and Banking Systems. BIS, December 2010 (revised June 2011).

Basel Committee on Banking Supervision Consultative Document. The New Basel Capital Accord. Bank for International Settlements, January 2001, issued for comment 31 May 2001.

Baudino, P., Goetschmann, R., Henry, J., Taniguchi, K., and Zhu, W. *Stress-Testing Banks – A Comparative Analysis*. FSI Insights on policy implementation No. 12. Financial Stability Institute BIS, November 2018.

BCBS Standard on Interest Rate Risk in the Banking Book. BIS, April 2016.

Beltratti, A. and Stulz, R.M. *Why Did Some Banks Perform Better During the Credit Crisis? A Cross-Country Study of the Impact of Governance and Regulation*. NBER Working Paper 15180, July 2009.

BIS Central Bank Survey of Foreign Exchange and Derivatives Market Activity. Bank for International Settlements, Monetary and Economic Department, May 1996.

Bitner, J.W. *Successful Bank Asset/Liability Management: A Guide to the Future Beyond Gap*. John Wiley & Sons, 1992.

Brewer, E., Minton, B., and Moser, J.T. *The Bank-Held Derivatives on Credit Accessibility*. Federal Reserve Bank of Chicago, Vol. 94–5, 1994, 208–28.

Brodt, A.I. Optimal Bank Asset and Liability Management with Financial Futures. *Journal of Futures Markets 8*(4), 1988, 457–64.

Carey, M. and Stulz, R.W. *The Risks of Financial Institution*. National Bureau of Economic Research Working Paper,June 2005, No. 11442.

Choudhry, M. *Bank Asset and Liability Management: Strategy, Trading, Analysis*. John Wiley & Sons, 2007.

Choudhry, M. *The Moorad Choudhry Anthology Past, Present and Future Principles of Banking and Finance*. Wiley, 2018.

Constâncio, V. *Challenges Faced by the European Banking Sector*. Speech at the Risk & Supervision Conference organized by Associazione Bancaria Italiana, Rome, 14 June 2017.

De Guindos, L. *Euro Area Banks: The Profitability Challenge*. speech at the ABI annual conference "Banking Union and Basel III – risk and supervision 2019," Rome, 25 June 2019.

ECB Guide to the Internal Capital Adequacy Assessment Process (ICAAP). EBA, November 2018.

ECB Guide to the Internal Liquidity Adequacy Assessment Process (ILAAP). EBA, November 2018.

ECBS Guiding Principles for the Operationalization of a Sectoral Countercyclical Capital Buffer. BCBS, 28 November 2019.

Edwards, F.R. and Mishkin, F.S. *The Decline of Traditional Banking: Implications for Financial Stability and Regulatory Policy*. National Bureau of Economic Research Working Paper, January 1995, No. 4993.

https://doi.org/10.1515/9783110669763-022

Enria, A. *Is Less More? Profitability and Consolidation in the European Banking Sector*. Presentation at the CIRSF Annual International Conference, Lisbon, 4 July 2019.
Enria, A. *Regulation, Proportionality and the Sustainability of Banking*. Speech at the Retail Banking Conference "Creating Sustainable Financial Structures by Putting Citizens First" of European Savings Bank Group. Brussels, 21 November 2019.
Final Guidelines on the Appropriate Subsets of Sectoral Exposures to Which Competent or Designated Authorities May Apply a Systemic Risk Buffer in Accordance with Article 133(5)(f) of Directive 2013/36/EU, EBA/GL/2020/13. EBA, 30 September 2020.
Final Report Guidelines on ICAAP and ILAAP Information Collected for SREP purposes, EBA/GL/2016/10. EBA, 3 November 2016.
Guide on the supervisory approach to consolidation in the banking sector. ECB, 12 January 2021.
Guidelines on the Application of the Supervisory Review Process under Pillar 2, (CP03 revised). CEBS, 25 January 2006.
Guidelines on Common Procedures and Methodologies for the Supervisory Review and Evaluation Process (SREP), EBA/GL/2014/13. EBA, 19 December 2014.
Guidelines on Common Procedures and Methodologies for the Supervisory Review and Evaluation Process (SREP) and Supervisory Stress Testing, EBA/GL/2014/13, 19 July 2018.
Guidelines on Internal Governance Under Directive 2013/36/EU, EBA/GL/2017/11. EBA, 26 September 2017.
Guidelines on Liquidity Cost Benefit Allocation. CEBS, October 2010.
Guidelines on the Management of Interest Rate Risk Arising from Non-Trading Activities. Final report, EBA/GL/2015/08. EBA, 22 May 2015.
Guidelines on the Management of Interest Rate Risk Arising from Non-Trading Book Activities, EBA/GL/2018/02. EBA, 19 July 2018.
Guidelines on the Treatment of Structural FX under Article 352(2) of Regulation (EU) No., 575/2013 (CRR), EBA/GL/2020/09. EBA, 1 July 2020.
Hakkarainen, P. *The EU Regulatory Environment – Room for Improvement*, speech at the Governance, Risk Management and Compliance conference, Frankfurt am Main, 19 November 2019.
Hesler, T., Laczkowski, K., and Roche,P. *Five Steps to a More Effective Global Treasury*. November 2011, http://www.mckinsey.com.
Introduction to the EMIR Technical Standards Based on the Regulation (EU) No 648/2012 on OTC Derivatives, CCPs and Trade Repositories. Financial Conduct Authority, 2013.
IFRS 3 Business Combinations, IFRS Standards.
IFRS 5 Non-Current Assets Held for Sale and Discontinued Operations, IFRS Standards.
IFRS 9 Financial Instruments, IFRS Standards.
Jeffery, E. *AT1 Capital/CoCo Bonds: What You Should Know*. Euromoney, July 15, 2019.
Joint ESMA and EBA Guidelines on the Assessment of the Suitability of Members of the Management Body and Key Function Holders under Directive 2013/36/EU and Directive 2014/65/EU, EBA/GL/2017/12, ESMA and EBA, 26 September 2017.
Kane, E.J. *Regulation and Supervision: An Ethical Perspective*. National Bureau of Economic Research Working Paper, March 2008, No. 13895.
Krishnamurthy, A., Bai, J., and Weymuller, Ch-H. *Measuring Liquidity Mismatch in the Banking Sector*. NBER Working Paper 22729, October 2016.
Laeven, L. and Levine, R. *Bank Governance, Regulation and Risk Taking*. National Bureau of Economic Research Working Paper, June 2008, No. 14113.
Leverage Ratio, BCBS, 15.12.2019.
Macauley, F.R. *Some Theoretical Problems Suggested by the Movements of Interest Yields, Bond Yields & Stock Prices in the United States Since 1856*, Reprint edition. Ayer Co. Pub., 1981.
Macrofinancial Stress-Testing – Principles and Practices. International Monetary Fund, August 2012.

Marshall, J.F. and Bansal, V.K. *Financial Engineering: A Complete Guide to Financial Innovation.* New York Institute of Finance, February 1, 1991.

Masuoka, T. *Asset and Liability Management in the Developing Countries: Modern Financial Techniques – A Primer.* World Bank Working Paper, June 1990, No. 454.

Mergaerts, F. and Vennet, R.V. Business Models and Bank Performance: A Long-Term Perspective. *Journal of Financial Stability 22*, 2016, 57–75.

Milestones in the History of U.S. Foreign Relations: OPEC Oil Embargo 1973–1974. Office of the Historian.

Minimum Requirement for Own Funds and Eligible Liabilities (MREL) SRB Policy under the Banking.

Mitchell, K. *Interest Rate Risk Management at Tenth Distinct Banks.* Economic Review, the Federal Reserve Bank of Kansas City, May 1985.

Neil, C. *An Introduction to Risk Management*, 2nd ed.. Prentice-Hall, 1986.

Package, SRB, 20.05.2020.

Polak, P. and Klusacek, I., *Centralization of Treasury Management.* Business Perspectives, 2010.

Policy Advice on the Basel III Reforms: Output Floor, EBA-Op-2019-09c. EBA, 2 August 2019.

Principles for Sound Stress Testing Practices and Supervision. BCBS, May 2009.

Ramirez, J., *Handbook Basel III capital Handbook of Basel III Capital. Enhancing Bank Capital in Practice*, John Wiley & Sons, 2016.

Redington F.M. Review of the Principles of Life Office Valuations. *Journal of the Institute of Actuaries 78*, 1952, 286–340.

Rogers, T.F. *The Government Securities Market: In the Wake of ESM.* Santa Clara, Rev. 587, 1987.

Rose, P. and Hudgins, S. *Bank Management & Financial Services*, 9th edition. McGraw Hill, 2013.

Sensitivity Analysis of Liquidity Risk – Stress Test 2019 Final Results. ECB, 7 October 2019.

Seventeenth Progress Report on Adoption of the Basel Regulatory Framework. BIS, October 2019.

Simons, K. Interest Rate Derivatives and Asset Liability Management by Commercial Banks. *New England Economic Review.* Federal Reserve Bank of Boston, January/February 1995, 17–28.

Sinkey, J.F. *Commercial Bank Financial Management in the Financial-Services Industry.* Prentice Hall, 2002.

Sinn, H.-W. *Risk Taking, Limited Liability and the Competition of Bank Regulators.* National Bureau of Economic Research Working Paper, December 2001, No. 8669.

Slovik, P. *Systemically Important Banks and Capital Regulations Challenges Economics Department.* Organization for Economic Cooperation and Development, 11 December 2012, No. 916, OECD ECO/WKP (2011)85.

SRB Expectations for Banks 2020, SRB, March 2020.

Standard on Asset-Liability Management, Standard No. 13. International Association of Insurance Supervisors, 2006.

Technical Aspects of the Management of Interest Rate Risk Arising from Non-Trading Activities under the Supervisory Review Process. CEBS, 3 October 2006.

The Application of Basel II to Trading Activities and the Treatment of Double Default Effects. BCBS, July 2005.

The Basel Committee's Response to the Financial Crisis: Report to the G20. Bank for International Settlements, October 2010.

Van Bunsbergen, J.H. and Brandt, M.W. *Optimal Asset Allocation in Asset Liability Management.* National Bureau of Economic Research Working Paper, March 2007, No. 12970.

Van Deventer, D.R. *Transfer Pricing Systems Design: Building Clarity in the Responsibility for and Measurement of Risk.* Kamakura Corporation, January 2002.

Weiner, E. and Fossaceca, M., Evolutions in Treasury Centralization. *Treasury & Risk Magazine.* June 13, 2013.

List of Figures

https://doi.org/10.1515/9783110669763-023

List of Tables

https://doi.org/10.1515/9783110669763-024

List of Abbreviations

ALCO	Asset and Liability Committee
ALM	Asset and Liability Management
ASF	Available Stable Funding
AT1	Additional Tier 1 Capital
BCBS	Basel Committee on Banking Supervision
BS	Balance Sheet
CAR	Capital Adequacy Ratio
CBR	Combined Buffer Requirement
CCB	Capital Conservation Buffer
CCS	Cross-Currency Swap
CCyB	Countercyclical Capital Buffer
CDS	Credit Default Swap
CEBS	Committee of European Banking Supervisors
CET1	Core Equity Tier 1
CoC	Cost of Capital
CRD	Capital Requirements Directive
CRR	Capital Requirements Regulation
EAD	Exposure at Default
EBA	European Banking Authority
ECB	European Central Bank
EL	Expected Loss
ES	Expected Shortfall
EVA	Economic Value Added
FDIC	Federal Deposit Insurance Corporation
FRTB	Fundamental Review of the Trading Book
FTP	Funds Transfer Pricing
ICAAP	Internal Capital Adequacy Assessment Process
IFRS	International Financial Reporting Standards
ILAAP	Internal Liquidity Adequacy Assessment Process
IRR	Interest Rate Risk
IRRBB	Interest Rate Risk in the Banking Book
IRS	Interest Rate Swap
KPI	Key Performance Indicator
LCR	Liquidity Coverage Ratio
LGD	Loss Given Default
LLP	Loan Loss Provisions
M&A	Mergers and Acquisitions
MREL	Minimum Requirement for Own Funds and Eligible Liabilities
NAV	Net Asset Value
NBER	National Bureau of Economic Research
NII	Net Interest Income
NIM	Net Interest Margin
NPL	Non-Performing Loans
NPV	Net Present Value
NSFR	Net Stable Funding Ratio
OCI	Other Comprehensive Income
OCP	Open Currency Position

https://doi.org/10.1515/9783110669763-025

OCR	Overall Capital Requirements
OPEX	Operating Expenses
P&L	Profit and Loss
P2G	Pillar 2 Guidance
P2R	Pillar 2 Requirement
PD	Probability of Default
RAS	Risk Appetite Statement
RoE	Return on Equity
RoRWA	Return on Risk Weighted Assets
RRP	Recovery and Resolution Planning
RSF	Required Stable Funding
RWA	Risk Weighted Assets
SRB	Single Resolution Board
SREP	Supervisory Review and Evaluation Process
SSM	Single Supervisory Mechanism
SyRB	Systemic Risk Buffer
T1	Tier 1 Capital
T2	Tier 2 Capital
TSCR	Total SREP Capital Ratio
VaR	Value-at-Risk

About the Author

Polina Bardaeva is an international asset and liability management (ALM) expert with 15 years of practical and theoretical experience in Treasury and banks' balance sheet steering. As a practitioner Polina was responsible for ALM in different types of banks: subsidiaries and head-offices, international and local, state-owned and private, in developing and developed markets. This multi-dimensional expertise gained at Absolut Bank (member of KBC Group in 2007–2011), MTS Bank, Sberbank of Russia and Sberbank Europe AG provided the basis for comparison of ALM in different circumstances and conclusions about applicability of best practices.

In academic activities the author of this book has been investigating virtues and drawbacks of historical concepts of ALM and feasibility of their application in practice. Polina Bardaeva holds a PhD in finance and banking (MSU, Russia) and is a certified financial risk manager (GARP, USA). Just after accomplishing her post-graduate studies Polina created an ALM course for master students and later was a co-founder of the Master of Financial Risk Management program at Lomonosov Moscow State University (Russia) and contributor to its cooperation with GARP.

Polina Bardaeva is an author and co-author of more than 20 publications (in Russian and in English) and a founding member of the faculty of the Certificate of Bank Treasury Risk Management professional qualification (London, UK).

https://doi.org/10.1515/9783110669763-026

Index

https://doi.org/10.1515/9783110669763-027

The Moorad Choudhry Global Banking Series

Principles of Green Banking: Managing Environmental Risk and Sustainability
by Suborna Barua

Reverse Stress Testing in Banking: A Comprehensive Guide
by Michael Eichhorn, Tiziano Bellini, and Daniel Mayenberger (eds.)

Bank Asset Liability Management Best Practice: Yesterday, Today and Tomorrow
by Polina Bardaeva

www.ingramcontent.com/pod-product-compliance
Lightning Source LLC
Chambersburg PA
CBHW080939240926
51849CB00004BA/497
* 9 7 8 3 1 1 0 6 6 6 5 4 0 *